"*Surviving and Thriving in Higher Education Professional Services* wonderfully discusses the theory and practice of professional services in universities, those essential and often overlooked colleagues who make higher education work. A great blend of pragmatism, advice, and anecdotes that should be essential reading for everyone who works in universities."

Professor Damien Page, *Deputy Vice-Chancellor, Buckinghamshire New University, UK*

"*Surviving and Thriving in Higher Education Professional Services* offers candid personal insights and practical guidance, demystifying career progression in HE. With actionable advice and an accessible style, it's an indispensable resource for HE professionals at any stage of their career."

Dr. Ella Popper, *Head of Professional Development, Association of Higher Education Professionals (AHEP), UK*

"Looking for a perfect blend of practical advice, vivid examples, and rich context? *Surviving and Thriving in Higher Education Professional Services* offers valuable insights and actionable steps, making complex concepts easy to grasp and apply in real-life situations."

Lesley O'Keeffe, *Registrar, Brunel University and Professional Development Lead for the Academic Registrars' Council (ARC), UK*

"Higher education is a challenging environment but offers great opportunities for a wide range of careers. *Surviving and Thriving in Higher Education Professional Services* skilfully describes how to navigate the complexities and work successfully with academic and other staff to deliver great results."

Dr. Paul Greatrix, *Registrar, University of Nottingham, UK*

"A must-read for anyone navigating the professional services landscape in UK HE. Rachel's empowering guide is packed with practical advice, real-life stories, and actionable strategies for achieving your career goals. Whether you're a newcomer or have been in the sector a while, add this to your bookshelf!"

Jonathan Dempsey, *Association of Higher Education Professionals (AHEP) Trustee, UK*

Surviving and Thriving in Higher Education Professional Services

Diving into the vibrant, challenging world of professional services in higher education, this empowering book provides tools to navigate complex structures, optimise mentorship, and thrive in a fulfilling career.

Whether you're a newcomer, a seasoned professional seeking advancement, or someone caught between academic and professional worlds, this book offers practical advice for success in UK higher education professional services. You'll learn strategies for navigating career paths, tackling change with confidence, cultivating a growth mindset, and developing strong communication, leadership, and problem-solving skills. Diverse stories from real-life professionals will guide you through a dynamic and unique career journey.

The guidance and advice within this comprehensive book will equip you with strategies for filling knowledge gaps, finding the right mentor, and fostering an inclusive team environment. Embrace challenges, build resilience, and unlock your full potential in the ever-evolving world of UK higher education professional services.

Rachel Reeds has been surviving and thriving in higher education professional services since 2011. An advocate of authentic leadership, she empowers others to find their voice, lead confidently, and take ownership of their professional journey.

Surviving and Thriving in Higher Education Professional Services

A Guide to Success

Rachel Reeds

LONDON AND NEW YORK

Designed cover image: © Getty Images

First published 2025
by Routledge
4 Park Square, Milton Park, Abingdon, Oxon OX14 4RN

and by Routledge
605 Third Avenue, New York, NY 10158

Routledge is an imprint of the Taylor & Francis Group, an informa business

© 2025 Rachel Reeds

The right of Rachel Reeds to be identified as author of this work has been asserted in accordance with sections 77 and 78 of the Copyright, Designs and Patents Act 1988.

All rights reserved. No part of this book may be reprinted or reproduced or utilised in any form or by any electronic, mechanical, or other means, now known or hereafter invented, including photocopying and recording, or in any information storage or retrieval system, without permission in writing from the publishers.

Trademark notice: Product or corporate names may be trademarks or registered trademarks, and are used only for identification and explanation without intent to infringe.

British Library Cataloguing-in-Publication Data
A catalogue record for this book is available from the British Library

ISBN: 978-1-032-86272-9 (hbk)
ISBN: 978-1-032-86269-9 (pbk)
ISBN: 978-1-003-52212-6 (ebk)

DOI: 10.4324/9781003522126

Typeset in Galliard
by codeMantra

This book is dedicated to those with voices yet to be heard. Voices too often unwanted, interrupted, or dismissed. Voices of wisdom, kindness, and innovation.

Keep speaking up. You will be heard.

Contents

Acknowledgements   *xiii*

Introduction   1
Why work in higher education professional services? 2
How did we end up here? 3
Why I wrote this book 4
What this book will do for you 4
Introducing the voices 5
About the author 6
This book is a starting point 8

1 **History, headlines, hierarchies: understanding UK higher education today**   10
A brief history of higher education in the UK 10
Current (and ongoing) debates 12
Organisation and oversight 15
'Us' and 'them' and in-between 17
Digging deeper 22

2 **Planning, progress, proficiency: navigating and succeeding in professional services**   25
A job or a career? 25
Getting started 30
Developing skills and knowledge 32
Setting goals 37
Believe in yourself 41
Digging deeper 42

3 Target, tailor, triumph: mastering the job search
    and interview   44
    The search 44
    A bit of background 44
    Your application 45
    The interview 48
    Afterwards 55
    Digging deeper 55

4 Strive, shine, soar: getting noticed and making
    a visible impact   56
    Be proactive 56
    Take initiative to solve problems and improve processes 61
    Learning from experienced professionals 64
    Demonstrating leadership skills 66
    Digging deeper 68

5 Empower, engage, elevate: managing people and teams   69
    Beginning 69
    Getting to know your team members 70
    Management manners 71
    Empowerment 79
    Confidence 82
    Digging deeper 85

6 Adapt, advocate, advance: embracing change
    and innovation   86
    Sector-wide change 86
    Innovation and influencing change locally 89
    Supporting your team through change 93
    Digging deeper 99

7 Navigate, nurture, negotiate: leading with confidence and
    tackling challenges   101
    *What's the difference between management
        and leadership? 101*
    Your leadership philosophy 102
    Dealing with difficult things 105
    The middle management sandwich 109
    Digging deeper 113

8   Reflect, refine, reimagine: cultivating personal and
    professional growth   114
    You are not 'too busy' 114
    Power of reflection 115
    Resilience 118
    Looking beyond 121
    Digging deeper 124

    Beyond survival: thriving in professional services   **125**
    LinkedIn is a great community for collaboration 125
    We shouldn't gate-keep knowledge 126
    We need to be confident and speak up 126
    Your commitment 126
    Your journey 127

    Index   *129*

Acknowledgements

A chorus of thanks goes out to the incredible community of professionals who so generously shared their experience, wisdom, and advice. I'm endlessly grateful for their candour, humour, and trust in me to share their stories.

I am grateful to everyone who championed this project. Whether it was a simple, 'Go for it!' or sharing thoughts, introductions, or a patient ear for my endless project chatter, their support means the world.

Special thanks to Bob Heads for his honest and insightful feedback on the first draft, and to Rebecca Collins for her editorial magic on the final draft.

Finally, my immense gratitude goes to Dr. Eleanor Reeds, Dr. Bethan Michael-Fox, and Magda Thomas. Without their unwavering support and belief, this book wouldn't exist.

Introduction

Think 'higher education' and what pops into most people's mind? Professors, students, textbooks, graduation ceremonies, lecture halls, libraries, and sports clubs, right? But the unseen heroes rarely come to mind. You know, the one who politely informed the accounting course leader their exciting new course couldn't be approved until modules added up to the required 120 credits per year? (Yep, that was me.) Or the admissions officer who meticulously combed through fee regulations, determined to find a way for an applicant to qualify for home fee status. The calm voice on the other end of the phone at the IT helpdesk, troubleshooting a virtual learning environment meltdown. The technician who makes sure the skills lab is always stocked with exactly what is needed for every session.

Beyond the familiar figure of the academic lecturer lies a vast, often unseen, army of professionals – the lifeblood of any higher education institution (HEI). There are over a quarter of a million of them in the UK (HESA, 2023). These individuals work across various universities, colleges, and other types of education providers. They are the folks in IT, finance, student support, libraries, academic registry, accommodation, recruitment, and countless other teams whose skills and expertise are as diverse and multi-faceted as their roles and responsibilities. In higher education they are known as Professional Services.

'Professional Services' is a broad and inherently complex label for those working in higher education in the UK and employed on contracts other than those defined as 'academic'. While in the USA and many other countries, higher education administration is seen as a respected profession, the label of 'administration' in the UK has many negative connotations so the sector has moved away from using it (Veles, Graham & Ovaska, 2023). When UK university league tables refer to staff–student ratios, by 'staff' they strictly refer to the 43 per cent of employees on academic contracts (HESA, 2023). Non-academic staff are professional practitioners and experts in their fields. Despite limited visibility in sector data and discourse, the truth is, HEIs would crumble without the professional staff forming the backbone of their very structures. (If you aren't sure, think of the chaos that would ensue if there was no timetabling team!)

DOI: 10.4324/9781003522126-1

We, professional services staff, are a passionate, though often overlooked group, muddling through a mix of rules, traditions, innovations, and government initiatives, at the same time as juggling limited resources. Often opportunities for training and development are scarce, which is ironic considering we work in institutions dedicated to teaching and learning. We're all doing our best, some with more experience than others, but most of us are simply 'winging it' with a smile and a coffee in hand. *(Personally, I prefer tea – Yorkshire, please, strong with a splash of milk – but I bow to peer pressure and include coffee as the representative caffeinated beverage here.)*

Higher education can feel like a labyrinth of acronyms, endless forms, and confusing hierarchies, but don't let that intimidate you. This book will guide you through this complex landscape. Whether you're actively pursuing a career in professional services within higher education, or simply stumbled onto this path unexpectedly, it is your starting point in navigating this sometimes-contradictory world.

Why work in higher education professional services?

It's funny how specific people and little moments can stick with you. Every now and then, something happens at work that reminds me why I love what I do. There was this international student I saw every week for a compliance check-in. About halfway through their second year of the social work degree, they walked in, tears streaming down their face. I sat with them, listening as they poured out their anxieties. They worried they weren't strong enough for social work, felt overwhelmed by the academic study, and were plagued by constant headaches. All I did was listen and then, when they seemed ready, I suggested we visit the student support team. 'Just see what they recommend', I said.

The next time they came in, it was like a whole new person walked through the door. They practically bounced into the office! The support team had booked them a session with a counsellor and arranged an assessment for learning difficulties. They had been given a diagnosis and some coloured glasses! The change was incredible. They were filled with such determination and optimism. That's the kind of moment that makes you realise the impact you can have, even in the smallest ways.

Higher education is a sector that offers diverse opportunities, intellectual stimulation, and the chance to make a real difference to the lives of students and the future of education. It encompasses a broad range of roles and potential career paths, each offering unique challenges and rewards, as part of a dynamic and intellectually stimulating environment.

We directly and indirectly contribute to the success of students and the sector by working on initiatives that enhance learning and development, student wellbeing, academic support services, or career development programmes. We facilitate world-leading research and innovation. Not only that, but we also empower and support our local communities through work in outreach, professional practice, and with businesses.

Compared to other sectors, HEIs in the UK often offer competitive salaries and benefits packages, including a reliable pension, and job security, making it a stable and rewarding career choice (jobs.ac.uk, 2024).

Many HEIs in the UK have unique missions and areas of focus. We can choose to work at an institution that aligns with our personal interests or values, allowing us to contribute to a specific cause we care about. I believe in the transformative power of education and choose to work in universities devoted to access rather than prestige. This keeps applicants, students, and the community at the heart of my professional practice.

Magda's perception of her colleagues' commitment demonstrates the passion many of us feel for our work:

> They feel proud about being part of this community. They feel proud about serving others and helping others progress. It strikes me as something almost noble.

A considerable number of people have long and fulfilling careers working in higher education. Joanne is one such person:

> You know what? We moan about it. But I love working in higher education. I love my job. It has been a long time since I've had the Sunday night scaries. A long time. And you can't ask for more than that.

How did we end up here?

I don't know anyone who works in higher education in a non-academic role who knew that it was what they wanted to do when they grew up. I certainly didn't. I had an abstract idea that I wanted to work in the public sector. When I was 17, and applying for university, I thought that because I wanted to do a history degree, I would be a teacher or work in a museum. I did not know what else I could do with my degree. Yet here I am.

Those 'accidental administrators' and professionals evolve into accidental managers (Lewis, 2014). The Chartered Management Institute (CMI) (2023) found 82 per cent of managers start leadership positions without any formal leadership or management training. I was one of those managers. None of us are quite sure how we ended up here, but we are committed to the sector and want to build a successful career. So, how can we succeed?

Most of what I have learnt has been by doing, observing, trying, and making mistakes, and by trying, reflecting, and trying again. It has not been learnt through formal qualifications and training. I have degrees in history and post-colonial studies – no practical people management or database navigation advice to be found there! It was only after I'd learnt much of what I know through experience – painful and positive – that I started the Association of Higher Education Professionals' (AHEP) Postgraduate Certificate in Higher Education Administration, Leadership and Management, which I completed in December 2023 – 12 years after I started working in higher education!

Why I wrote this book

This is the book I wish I'd had when I was first starting out in higher education and when I first starting line managing people. It covers everything I fumbled through learning the hard way.

There are lots of books, guides, podcasts, and talks that cover career progression, leadership, and management. Most of them either assume a lot of knowledge, relate to the (American) private sector, or are pitched at senior leaders. There isn't much for those of us on the ground working with limited resources and very little training or support.

There are scores of books for academics in higher education looking for support in developing their teaching and research skills, but I had to search for a long time to find anything for professional services officers and managers in the UK. My frustration with the lack of accessible resources and information inspired me to write this book. My aim was to bring together the information, advice, and guidance that I felt was lacking when I needed it.

What this book will do for you

This book will be your introductory guide to thriving and progressing in UK higher education. It will delve into the real, dynamic world of HEIs, exploring the diversity of roles, squiggly career paths, and potential opportunities that await. It is relevant for those just starting out in higher education – at whatever stage of your career journey that might be, entry or senior management – and for those looking for practical advice to fill gaps in their knowledge, plan their next steps, and deal with challenges. It will help you build momentum in a successful and fulfilling career, within the unique context of professional services in UK higher education.

You'll discover:

- How to get to grips with your first job in higher education professional services, understand complex structures and overcome challenges with confidence.
- How to build a solid foundation for progression, developing essential skills like communication, leadership and problem-solving, while identifying your ideal role through self-evaluation and goal setting.
- Strategies for navigating the murky waters of professional development, maximising learning opportunities, finding trusted mentors, and proactively seeking out opportunities to shine.

- The inside scoop on landing your next role, from crafting a winning application to acing the interview and taking the reins with confidence.
- Essential guidance for leading a team, fostering inclusivity, managing change with confidence, and supporting your team through difficult situations and unexpected challenges.
- The key to evolving from manager to leader, tackling complex issues like performance management and conflict, and navigating the unique pressures of middle management.
- The power of continuous personal growth, mastering reflective practice, building resilience, and cultivating the mindset of a lifelong learner.

Introducing the voices

Throughout this book, a diverse group of higher education professionals share their journeys and offer guidance on your higher education career path. Here are the people you will meet through these pages.

David Duell is Head of Operations at the University of Birmingham. He believes in a strong, positive network, in communicating honestly and openly (and with a little humour), and in paying things forward. He is unashamedly passionate about UK higher education as a sector in which to work and is energised and motivated by self-development and supporting others in their professional development.

David Fryer is Head of Web and User Experience at Cranfield University. His interests and skills took him initially into a career in marketing. His morals and values then led him into the higher education sector where he has worked since 2012. He feels very strongly about empowering others to be creative and innovative.

Jeanette Eriksson is Head of Admissions at the University of Portsmouth and an experienced leadership coach. Having grown up in Sweden, she studied her undergraduate degree in London. She brings her own brand of Scandinavian sensibility to her professional practice.

Jenny James worked in course administration for 14 years before moving into a role in governance at the Open University in 2016. She initially didn't think she had anything helpful to contribute to this project, in her own words, 'as I have no ambition and like to stay in the same job for 25 years!' In fact, she has lots to share. She offers her unique perspective on finding work rewarding despite not looking for promotion and working part-time hours.

Joanne Caldwell is the School Business Manager in the Salford Business School at the University of Salford. She recently completed a doctorate in education, focusing on the relationship between professional services and academics. She is particularly interested in identity and challenging the traditional academic/professional services divide.

Julie Tysoe is an experienced programme and project manager and change practitioner. She is highly skilled at business process improvement, managing portfolios of strategic change in service of institutional strategy, managing complex operational environments, and leading transformative change projects in higher education.

Magda Thomas moved to the UK after finishing her teaching degree in Poland. She knew no one and had no job or income. She is now Executive Relationships Coordinator at the University of Strathclyde Business School in Glasgow. She has made many bold changes in her life and career (she calls them 'tiger jumps') and believes strongly that being open-minded is key to success and satisfaction.

Mehmet Tarhan's first job at London South Bank University was requesting references for applications to research degree courses for 35 hours a week. He is now Head of Market Planning and Insight where he oversees new student number planning, the customer relationships management (CRM) team and the market research team. He is a forward-looking, strategic thinker who brings together data and strategy in a unique way that has hugely benefited his institution.

Peter Wolstencroft is passionate about ensuring access to high-quality education and a positive learning experience for all. He works in the Business School at Manchester Metropolitan University, but he told me he knows 'nothing about business, so I always feel as though I'm a complete fraud, because my entire job is making sure that the teaching and the learning goes smoothly'. He shares his perspective as an academic mediating between academic and professional services colleagues.

Sarah Meir joined higher education administration after many years working in marketing in the financial services sector. She is University Executive Manager in the Business School at Liverpool Hope University. She feels strongly about supporting 'accidental administrators' in their professional development to succeed wherever they might go in their careers.

Simon Herbertson is a School Business Manager at the University of Salford where he has worked since 2001. Having initially worked as a primary school teacher, he started at Salford as a temporary secretary as a means of gaining administrative experience without any real idea of his next steps. He has successfully built his career by taking advantage of opportunities and building strong relationships across the university.

The extracts from transcripts of oral interviews with these contributors (the 'voices' you will hear throughout) have been edited but every effort has been taken to reflect the intention of each person. Each contributor has reviewed the edited extracts and consented to the words used.

The contributors' professional affiliations are correct at the time of publication but as careers shift this information may no longer be accurate. LinkedIn profiles will reflect current professional settings.

About the author

And then there's me, **Rachel Reeds**. I had one intention when I left university – to work in a role that served the community. I started out as a democratic services officer in a small district council. I believed in what I was doing in principle – supporting the decision-making functions of local government – but over time, that belief started to unravel. The decisions I facilitated, the reports I wrote, felt uncomfortable. The politics of the local authority I was serving didn't align with my values, and the sound of the disconnect grew louder and louder. It was something I couldn't ignore.

Serving the community was still my passion, but the political environment in which I worked felt stifling. I craved an environment driven by empowerment and accessibility, not politicking and exclusivity. Higher education, with its focus on learning and growth, resonated with me. My local government skills – wrangling paperwork, communicating effectively, building relationships, and negotiating – seemed like a good fit.

But the path to higher education wasn't paved with acceptance letters. The rejections piled up, each one chipping away at my confidence. Was this a dead end? Was I taking a wrong turn? Maybe I should find a job in local government in a less conservative council. Then, after one interview, the panel chair offered a parting suggestion: 'The Business School needs a quality assurance officer'. I had zero quality assurance experience, didn't really understand the job description, and didn't think I had any chance of getting the role. I applied anyway and did secure the job.

The quality officer role turned out to be my gateway into professional services in higher education. The skills I'd learnt in local government stood me in good stead and proved their worth. Regulations, reports, writing minutes, negotiating with people with important role titles – it all made sense. However, the transition wasn't easy. The academic jargon and institutional culture were confusing at first. But I adapted, finding my way through trial and error, experimentation and frustration, determination and hard work.

With that role, I started working in a university in one of the most diverse towns in the UK. I spent the first few years of my higher education career unlearning everything I thought I knew about how the world worked from my sheltered, comfortable youth. It was at this time that I completed an MA in Culture, Diaspora, Ethnicity at Birkbeck College, University of London, to try and make sense of the world as my newly opened eyes were experiencing it.

Since joining higher education in 2011, I've worked in course approvals, taught and research course administration, and admissions. I am passionate about fair and inclusive admissions and empowering applicants and my team members to make confident choices about their futures. I am simultaneously a computer nerd (I never imagined I'd need to learn to code to work in admissions) and a reflective thinker. I question everything. I'm sure this is a bit annoying for others at times, but I'm proud to be a positive disruptor. More recently I completed a Postgraduate Certificate in Higher Education Administration, Management and Leadership which has helped me to develop my professional practice as a leader.

In this book, I share my journey and what I have learnt along the way. As we all are, I am very much a product of my own experiences, background, and education. I offer only what I have learnt along my professional journey in higher education. My values, philosophy, attitude, and approach have been greatly influenced by my interactions – positive and negative, empowering and difficult – with people: colleagues, managers, mentors, tutors, friends, foes, students, politicians, and organisational partners.

This book reflects the experience of a community of practice. It is a guide to support professional development rather than prescriptive career and leadership advice. It can't cover everything. It has been designed so you can dip in and out depending on what you are looking for or what stage of your professional journey you are at. Some parts may resonate deeply with you, while others may seem less relevant.

This book is a starting point

There is so much that is wonderful about working in higher education, but some parts are harder than others. This book guides you through some of the more challenging parts so you can find satisfaction and success in your career. If you don't know where to start, start here.

The first chapter offers an introduction to the history of higher education in the UK, current debates, organisation and oversight, and the academic-professional binary. This is followed by a chapter exploring the core skills required to succeed in professional services, how to develop them, goal setting, and professional development planning. This forms a foundation for the chapter on mastering the job search which takes you through the entire application and interview process.

Chapter 4 covers how to get noticed. It explores how to build a professional profile, take initiative, demonstrate leadership skills, and secure mentorship as means to progress your career. Acknowledging that people management – whether through line management, supervision, coordination, or project responsibility – is fundamental to progressing into a higher-grade role in professional services, Chapter 5 offers an introduction to the skills and knowledge you will need to build competence and confidence as a team leader. It covers where to start, communication, inclusivity, empowerment, trust, confidence, and building supportive networks. A chapter on embracing change and innovation walks you through what drives change across the sector, how to keep up to date, how to influence change locally, and how to support your team through change.

Building on the portfolio of skills explored through the chapters so far, Chapter 7 covers philosophies of leadership, dealing with difficult things (from poor performance to conflict within teams), the middle management 'sandwich', and diplomacy. The last chapter challenges you to explore reflective practice, offers strategies to build resilience, and explores opportunities beyond a new role. This book concludes with a practical exercise to support you in planning your next steps for moving forward confidently in your career journey.

For those of you wanting to dig deeper, each chapter concludes with some prompts and questions for reflection. This is followed by details of the materials referenced in the chapter and resources for further research (blogs, podcasts, mailing lists, books, and websites).

Higher education is a sector that is constantly changing. You are advised to ensure you confirm the most up-to-date information regarding policy and practice and follow your institutional processes.

Irrespective of your background, experience, or current role, I hope that within these pages you'll find the tools, knowledge, and encouragement you need to carve your own path, unlock your potential, and thrive in the vibrant world of higher education.

References

CMI, 2023. New study: bad managers and toxic work culture causing one in three staff to walk. *CMI*, 16 October. Available at: <www.managers.org.uk/about-cmi/media-centre/press-releases/bad-managers-and-toxic-work-culture-causing-one-in-three-staff-to-walk/>.

HESA, 2023. Statistical bulletin 264: higher education staff statistics: UK, 2021/22. *HESA*, 17 January. Available at: <www.hesa.ac.uk/news/17-01-2023/sb264-higher-education-staff-statistics>.

Jobs.ac.uk, 2024. A snap shot of the benefits of working at a university. *Jobs.ac.uk*. Available at: <https://career-advice.jobs.ac.uk/career-development/a-snap-shot-of-the-benefits-of-working-at-a-university/>.

Lewis, K., 2024. Constructions of professional identity in a dynamic higher education sector. *Perspectives: Policy and Practice in Higher Education*, 18(2), pp. 43–50. https://doi.org/10.1080/13603108.2014.914107.

Veles, N., Graham, C. and Ovaska, C., 2023. University professional staff roles, identities, and spaces of interaction: systematic review of literature published in 2000–2020. *Policy Reviews in Higher Education*, 7(2), pp. 127–168. https://doi.org/10.1080/23322969.2023.2193826.

Chapter 1

History, headlines, hierarchies
Understanding UK higher education today

In this chapter, I introduce the UK higher education sector, exploring its rich history, the current debates shaping its future, and the key structures that hold it all together. This is followed by an overview of the significant developments that transformed the landscape, including the introduction of tuition fees and the recent push towards sustainability. Current debates on affordability, the relevance of curriculums, social mobility, and the increasing focus on international students are outlined.

Understanding the structures and hierarchies that govern these institutions is crucial. We will unpack important roles, committee structures, and the complex web of reporting lines.

No exploration of UK higher education is complete without examining the relationship between academic and professional services staff. We will explore beyond the traditional 'us and them' divide, considering the emergence of blended identities and the ongoing conversations about collaboration.

This chapter equips you with a comprehensive understanding of UK higher education, its past, present and the ongoing discussions that will shape its future.

A brief history of higher education in the UK

The history of higher education in the UK is a topic that lots of people working in higher education know little about. I certainly didn't. A lot of strategic and political decisions make more sense once you have a basic comprehension of the history of higher education in the UK. This brief overview will give you a broad understanding and explain some of the hierarchies and politics between different groups of higher education institutions (HEIs).

A long time ago (12th–18th centuries)

During this time, the Church of England held a monopoly on higher education in England, with Oxford and Cambridge (Oxbridge) the only centres of higher learning offering courses in theology, classics, and philosophy.

Access was strictly limited to the elite, primarily men from wealthy families. Scottish universities offered a slightly broader curriculum, including law and medicine, but still only to men.

The Victorians (19th century)

The Industrial Revolution and growing scientific advancements sparked a demand for education beyond the classics. University College London (UCL) (1826) and King's College London (1829) emerged as secular alternatives to Oxbridge, offering subjects like engineering and medicine. The 'redbrick' universities (Manchester and Birmingham, for example) challenged the dominance of Oxbridge, with a focus on practical knowledge, catering to the needs of the rising industrial class. During this time, the University of Edinburgh (1869) and new women's colleges like Girton (1869) and Bedford (1878) opened their doors to female students who had previously been excluded from higher education. The 1870 Education Act introduced free, compulsory primary education, laying the groundwork for wider participation in education more broadly.

Democratisation and diversification (20th century)

To meet the demands of a modern economy, the Robbins Report (1963) advocated for mass higher education. During this period, many new universities and colleges were established across the country, with a focus on technological and vocational training. Polytechnics (Loughborough and Bradford, for example) provided practical education for working-class students, often specialising in science, engineering, and business. While participation increased, disparities persisted, with students from lower socioeconomic backgrounds less likely to attend university.

Globalisation and commercialisation (late 20th and early 21st centuries)

The 1992 Further and Higher Education Act abolished the divide between universities and polytechnics, granting university status to many of the latter (that became known as post-1992 universities). This doubled the number of universities, diversifying the landscape and increasing access, particularly for vocational fields. Student fees were introduced in 1998, leading to concerns about affordability of full-time undergraduate study and increasing debt burdens. The 21st century witnessed further expansion, with the UK higher education entry rate for 18 years olds (i.e., school and college leavers) peaking at 38.2 per cent in 2021 (Bolton, 2024). International recruitment, transnational education (TNE), and overseas campuses became central to most universities' long-term strategies.

There has been a growth in alternate provision, including higher education in further education (degree-level study delivered in further education colleges and validated by universities), private universities, and degree apprenticeships.

Current (and ongoing) debates

This is a non-exhaustive introduction to the big issues and challenges that are constantly being debated across the sector.

Money

The affordability of university study remains at the top of the political and social agenda. The introduction of tuition fees and the withdrawal of most grants in 1998 significantly changed the funding landscape. Supporters argue it increased university autonomy and diversified funding sources, while critics highlight rising debt and deterrents to students from disadvantaged backgrounds.

Debates continue to rage surrounding the adequacy of student loans, especially considering the cost-of-living crisis. Issues of regional and socio-economic disparities in access to financial support also remain under scrutiny. This includes the different support available across the four nations of the UK and to those seeking postgraduate loans (introduced in 2016). A new Lifelong Learning Entitlement framework for funding re-engineers the loan framework to encompass more flexible and modular provision. However, initial indications are that the changes may not address many of the existing barriers to funding (particularly as most distance-learning provision is excluded) (Khandekar, 2023).

Some people argue for increased public investment to combat rising costs and ensure equitable access, while others advocate for further diversifying funding through public-private partnerships or philanthropic initiatives.

Undergraduate full-time tuition fees have been frozen at £9250 since 2017. While students struggle with the cost of studying full-time and significant student debt upon graduation, HEIs are increasingly relying on other income sources (international recruitment, commercial partnerships) to balance their books whilst being challenged about the value-for-money of undergraduate degrees. Students are defined as 'customers' under consumer law but they aren't automatically entitled to get what they think they are paying for, in other words, a degree (CMA, 2023). Managing expectations, meeting students' needs, and being commercially competitive are an ongoing challenge.

Curriculum relevance and employability

Concerns exist about aligning degree courses with the needs of the modern workforce. This focus has created a focus on ensuring graduates are equipped with the skills and experience they need to succeed in the workforce, rather than see degree-level study as a purely academic, intellectual endeavour. Currently, there is pressure to incorporate digital skills, entrepreneurship, and interdisciplinary approaches to enhance graduate employability. The need for flexible, accessible learning pathways beyond traditional degrees (often referred to as lifelong learning) is increasingly recognised. This includes exploring online learning, micro-credentials, and upskilling opportunities to cater to a dynamic and rapidly evolving job market and expectations from students of greater flexibility (often for financial reasons). Balancing theoretical knowledge with practical skills training is a constant challenge for HEIs. This is the vocational versus academic debate. The debate revolves around enhancing vocational pathways while maintaining the core academic strengths of HEIs. Degree apprenticeships and Higher Technical Qualifications (HTQs) are products of this discussion.

Social mobility and widening access

Despite increased overall participation, concerns remain about unequal access to higher education for students from socially and economically disadvantaged backgrounds, ethnic minorities, care leavers, students with a disability, and students from rural areas. The debate surrounds implementing effective outreach programmes, tackling financial barriers, and addressing systemic inequalities in education prior to entering higher education. Scotland's approach is quite different from that of the rest of the UK. Scotland takes a whole sector approach rather than leaving it to individual organisations to implement individual strategies (Universities Scotland, 2024). In England and Wales each HEI decides its own approach.

The need for reforms to the undergraduate admissions processes to move beyond a reliance on exam results keeps being raised. Factors like socioeconomic context and potential are recognised as key but no one has yet come up with a commercially and politically acceptable alternative to the current system of prospective application based on achieved and predicted grades.

Ensuring adequate support systems for students from disadvantaged backgrounds is crucial for retention and success. This includes academic, financial, and pastoral support tailored to their specific needs. All HEIs have an action plan (in England referred to as an Access and Participation Plan (APP) to meet their internal and external targets for increasing participation in higher education and improving student outcomes. However, league tables (rankings) continue to carry significant weight for funding allocation and applicant decision-making with over 75 per cent of UK league table metrics are negatively related to widening participation (Hubbard, O'Neill & Nattrass, 2021). Making progress in one often compromises the other.

Globalisation and internationalisation

Attracting and retaining international students is vital for HEIs, both financially and culturally. However, concerns exist about potential exploitation, ensuring ethical recruitment practices and restrictions imposed by government immigration policy. The restriction placed on student visas (with applicants no longer being permitted to sponsor dependents to bring with them, such as family members) from January 2024 is the latest regulatory change to have a significant impact on higher education recruitment and, therefore, the financial viability of HEIs in the UK. The availability, or lack of, post-study work visas has a significant influence on the attractiveness of UK higher education to international students and is subject to changes in government policy over time.

Increased global mobility of students and academics, and overseas campuses, raise questions about collaboration versus competition between HEIs. Balancing national interests with internationalisation is an important challenge.

Academic standards on entry and exit

Debates continue about academic standards, quality of degrees being awarded, and how to achieve or maintain equity across the sector. Foundation years and entry requirements (advertised and actual) are always under the magnifying glass in the press and government. Reviews of Level 3 qualifications – of which there is a broad range, currently including A-levels, BTECs, T-levels, the Welsh Baccalaureate, Scottish Highers, the E-bacc, Advanced Apprenticeships, Cambridge Technical diplomas, and many more – continue. The debate ebbs and flows with policy and priority. The University and Colleges Admissions Service's (UCAS) tariff system is designed to ensure equity of consideration of different qualifications by offering a single standardised metric for assessing UK qualifications.

Sustainability

Sustainable development is an increasing global priority, with a focus on social, environmental, and financial sustainability across the higher education sector.

There has been a move towards conceptualising higher education under the umbrella of 'tertiary' education rather than separating it from further and vocational education as boundaries between become increasingly blurred (for example, degree apprenticeships). It is not dissimilar from previous dialogue which referred to 'post-compulsory' education.

Student wellbeing

HEIs are increasingly focused on, and expected to be actively working to support, student wellbeing both on and off campus. The University Mental

Health Charter programme was launched in 2019 (Hughes & Spanner, 2019). The 2023 Access and Participation Plan guidance includes a new, explicit requirement for English HEIs to "consider…how they can improve the mental health of their students" as poor mental health can impact successful qualification outcomes (OfS, 2023b). Financial challenges faced by students are negatively impacting their wellbeing in a multitude of ways, from requiring students to work more hours alongside their studies to the impact of poor-quality housing on their physical health (Brown, 2024).

Organisation and oversight

Every HEI has a board of governors that oversees its activity, ensuring financial solvency and the effective use of resources. From that level down, there exists a complex family tree.

There are a number of roles for senior staff in HEIs that are unusual and not seen outside higher education. Here are a few of the most common across the sector:

Chancellor: The ceremonial figurehead. Often seen at graduation ceremonies wearing an elaborate gown.
Vice-Chancellor/Principal: The 'CEO' of the HEI and the operational leader.
Pro/Deputy Vice-Chancellors (PVCs/DVCs)/Deputy Principals: Deputies with specific portfolios of responsibility, such as international strategy or academic research.
University Secretary: Responsible for governance. Often supports the work of the HEI's Senate/Council.
Dean: Academic leader of a faculty (subject-oriented group of departments/schools). Supported by an array of deputy/sub/associate deans.
Registrar: Senior manager responsible for the academic administration of students in areas such as enrolment, student records and course data.

The organisational structures usually follow a linear family tree model, starting at the position of Vice-Chancellor/Principal, down through Deputy/Pro Vice-Chancellors and Deans, heads of service, senior managers, team leaders to officers at the bottom. Some organograms feature 'dotted lines' crossing some of these silos and boundaries. 'Dotted lines' are relationships that are hard to define, not least for those who are subject to them. They usually refer to some form of accountability or consultative relationship. It can be helpful to get (written) clarity on what is required by each reporting line and to ensure there are no contradictions or conflicts between expectations. Simon's experience is probably similar to many:

> We had a solid line to director of school operations and a dotted line into our schools and to our deans. But the deans were unhappy with that. Now

we have a solid line to our deans, and our dotted line has gone to a role that no longer exists, so I don't know who our dotted line is to anymore!

It is characteristic of higher education that decision-making is simultaneously collaborative and argumentative. Academic independence, innovation, regulation, policy, and process make for a challenging combination. The result is lots of committees and a lot of people unsure about how the committees work. Committees come in many forms in higher education: boards, sub-committees, working groups, special interest groups, and panels. Working out the relationships between committees and where to take a proposal to get it approved can be tricky if your institution doesn't have a document outlining the committee structure.

Accountability

The **Office for Students (OfS)** is England's current regulator of higher education. It maintains a register of HEIs in England. HEIs are required to demonstrate that they have met certain requirements to become registered and have to meet specified obligations to remain registered (conditions of registration). Registration is a requirement for accessing public money (student loans funding), awarding degrees, and sponsoring student visas (OfS, 2022). The conditions of registration aim to ensure that:

- Everyone has a fair chance at attending, regardless of their background.
- The education is high-quality and effective, with clear standards and good outcomes for all students.
- Students are treated well, and their rights are protected.
- Institutions are financially stable and can deliver their courses as promised.
- They are well-managed and accountable.
- Students get all the information they need to make informed choices.
- Fees and funding are used responsibly.

The other nations of the UK have their own regulatory bodies: the **Scottish Funding Council (SFC)**, the **Commission for Tertiary Education and Research (CTER)** in Wales, and the **Department for the Economy** in Northern Ireland.

All these regulators are informed by data collected from HEIs across the UK by HESA (Higher Education Statistics Agency) and hold HEIs accountable for their actions and the outcomes of their students.

HEIs are accountable to multiple other stakeholders. These include accrediting bodies (such as the Nursing & Midwifery Council (NMC) for pre-registration nursing and midwifery courses), other funding providers (such as the Education and Skills Funding Council (ESFA) for degree apprenticeships in England), Ofsted (for apprenticeships and teacher training), students, parents and business partners including UCAS and government bodies.

In addition to the regulators the Quality Assurance Agency (QAA) reviews standards and quality in higher education across the UK. It is also the regulator of the Access to Higher Education diploma, which offers an alternative route to higher education for those without traditional qualifications. In the UK, QAA subject benchmark statements serve as important guidelines for universities and colleges to develop, deliver and review their academic programmes (QAA, 2024). The QAA UK Quality Code for Higher Education (2023) encapsulates the expectations for standards and quality of provision of the higher education sector.

Collaboration between universities

There are organisations and groups through which HEIs collaborate and partner. For example, Universities UK (UUK) (2024), with Universities Scotland and Universities Wales, brings together over 140 universities across the UK to collaborate and influence policy. It works across divisions, such as mission group membership, UCAS entry tariff group (high, medium, or low), history, and region.

Mission groups are coalitions of universities and colleges with shared aims, characteristics, and priorities (Lazell, 2024). They are the Russell Group, MillionPlus, University Alliance, GuildHE, and the Cathedrals Group.

The TEF-REF space

In UK higher education, the Teaching Excellence Framework (TEF) and Research Excellence Framework (REF) wield considerable influence. The TEF, introduced in 2017, assesses undergraduate teaching through metrics like student outcomes and satisfaction, awarding gold, silver or bronze ratings that are designed to guide student choices and, in England, affect the level of tuition fee that can be charged (OfS, 2023a). The REF, on the other hand, rigorously evaluates research quality and impact every six years, allocating funding based on expert-assessed grades (REF, 2024). While both play crucial roles, their influence isn't without limitations.

The TEF's limitations include its reliance on limited metrics, potentially undervaluing diverse teaching styles, and overlooking factors like institutional context. Likewise, the REF focuses on quantifiable outputs, potentially undervaluing innovative research that defies easy measurement. Additionally, both frameworks are resource intensive for HEIs, potentially diverting focus from core activities. Despite these limitations, the TEF and REF are central to higher education operations in the UK.

'Us' and 'them' and in-between

Academics (those doing the teaching and/or research) and professional staff (those doing the other stuff) are often presented as operating in separate bubbles. They bump into each other at intervals and things get passed between them: grades, feedback, problems, and information about students. University strategies like to refer to partnerships between academics and professional services as if they are separate entities. There are usually distinct hierarchies for each. There can be tensions that come from differing priorities, expectations, perceived status, and cultures. The 'us' and 'them' polarity keeps popping up. There are academics and then there is everyone else, the 'non-academics'.

It's an age-old binary that permeates the sector. It's entrenched in the sector's culture and long history. HESA's definitions of academic and non-academic clearly illustrate the established division and imbalance in profile between the role groups. It states, 'academic staff contracts are for planning, directing and undertaking academic teaching and research…Non-academic staff contracts include managers, professionals in non-academic jobs, student welfare workers, secretaries, caretakers and cleaners' (HESA, 2024). Academics first to be defined and described by what they do, while everyone else is defined by their job title and/or what they are not. Note the additional choice to list roles in order of descending pay grade.

Despite working at the same institution with shared goals, academics and professional staff can struggle to connect due to expectations of difference and differing expectations. Academics may feel their work and priorities are not fully grasped by professional staff, leading to impatience and criticism. Conversely, professional staff might perceive themselves as undervalued and disrespected by academics, who they view as isolated and out of touch. This tension extends to tensions between faculties (academic territory) and centralised teams (professional services). This dynamic creates a sense of working in separate worlds, impeding collaboration, and potentially hindering the HEI's overall success (Hobson et al., 2018).

Contractual differences

There are fundamental differences between the contracts of academic and professional staff in UK HEIs. HESA (2023) only requires HEIs to submit data on people employed on academic contracts in England and Northern Ireland (except the Vice-Chancellor). As if any such organisation could function without the scores of other staff who don't fall into that category! This reinforces the invisibility of the contribution of professional staff.

But what's an academic? That's a good a question. An academic is broadly someone engaged in teaching and/or research. But a technician in a research lab isn't classed an academic, nor is someone teaching study skills to students through library services. Ultimately, it comes down to the contract. Academic and 'non-academic' employment contracts, terms, conditions, and privileges sustain the embedded structural divide between 'us' and 'them' reflecting social, cultural, and organisational differences (Caldwell, 2024). Joanne finds it extremely frustrating:

> This is my big bugbear: all the contracts do is define your annual leave, your salary and sometimes it defines your pension. That's literally all it does. I do as many, or if not more, hours than an academic, and yet they are rewarded. Not salary wise, but they are certainly rewarded in terms of more annual leave than I get, for no reason. And I think we are never going to get away from that inequality until we start looking at reasons why. But I think we are so steeped in this historic notion of them and us.

I deliberately use the term professional services to refer to those of us who broadly fall outside the domain of 'doing' research and teaching. This replaces terms such as administrators, non-academic staff, or support staff. I do that consciously. It reflects the evolution in the identity of such staff members and the variety of skills and professionalisms encompassed by it. Equally, it is a reaction against some of the negative feelings those terms invoke in those of us badged by them. Most particularly the label of 'admin', of which Sarah is not a fan:

> In the UK, the word admin is quite a derogatory term, whereas in Europe and America it's a highly skilled thing.

In terms of lived experience, the binary is not so clear cut. Professional identities evolve. While some professional staff are gaining academic credentials, some academics are becoming more project-focused and spending time away from the TEF-REF space. A doctoral graduate or early career researcher has many options within higher education, not just the traditional pathways through lecturing. Similarly, a course administrator does not have to remain within Registry (academic services). We are working on projects outside and across traditional academic or administrative roles. We are being more collaborative and interdependent. Such broad initiatives cover areas including learning technology, student wellbeing, community outreach, apprenticeships, outreach, and business partnerships.

It can be helpful to think of it as a continuum. The professor is at one end, conducting research, supervising research students, and teaching degree programmes. The traditional student support-based professional services are at the other end. These include student records administration, student services, admissions, and finance. In many ways, no one is quite sure where the boundaries lie between the traditional academic and non-academic camps. In between lie those who feel that they don't belonging to either. They populate a space both between, and in, both camps. These blended, or multi, professionals have responsibilities and identities that include elements of academic and professional services activity (Whitchurch, 2008). Subject technicians, learning technologists, librarians, and research funding officers might feel they occupy this space. They exist across, and between, traditional boundaries, disrupting traditional divisions. For example, a research funding officer works directly with academic staff, writes funding bids, and negotiates with research centres. Technology is a dominant factor in this space as the interaction of technology and learning has created new roles and new skill sets (White, White & Borthwick, 2021).

But the cultural and structural division remains deeply entrenched, even though it is blurring. The labels are also important to people in terms of their professional identity (Barnett & Di Napoli, 2008).

Tensions and power imbalances

The relationships between academic and professional staff, and between faculties and centralised services, are nuanced and complex. They are formed, sustained, and altered by interactions between staff, policy, contracts, reporting lines, budget oversight, and a myriad of other factors.

Despite, or because of, embedded institutional and historic hierarchies, the interdependence between academic and professional staff can be a point of tension as well as cooperation. The principle that Sarah lays out to her team of administrators reflects this:

> Do your job. Help them to do theirs, but don't do theirs for them.

Job titles can cause some confusion, with the various roles being unclear to those on the 'outside' (i.e., not in professional services/a particular HEI) finding it difficult to understand the scope, level of responsibility, and purpose of a role (Melling, 2019). There are also sustained imbalances in workload whereby academics and professional service staff can both feel disadvantaged. I've had to point out to many academics complaining they didn't have enough hours in their workload plan for the extra interviews 'admissions' needed them to do, that it's the applicants who need the interviews and there is no system of workload planning for professional services staff, so we could end up being worse off in terms of extra workload!

Sarah illustrates how this imbalance can play out day to day:

> Personal administration sits in that bit in the middle of the continuum as the academics don't want to do their own personal administration. So I have to try to help my administrators understand that this is our job and that is theirs. We are a team and therefore we all have to do our own part. There are things that interlink in the middle, but we need to focus on this bit and help and train them to do their own bit. So when they go, 'I don't know where this is', don't send them the document, send them the link and get them to find it themselves. Help them to help themselves.

Adding value is actually what we should be doing. So think about how to say no to some things, how to push some things back so that they are more appropriate to the role. Because you're only allowed to do this much, you're only paid to do this much. You are grade fours, grade fives, they are sevens and eights. Think about that.

David D. shared an example of this tendency of academic staff to lean excessively on junior professional services staff:

I came in this entry level admin role, which was department administrator and PA to the head of an academic department. There were initially about 45 academics so it was a chunky department within a business school and all of the usual stuff that you would expect: helping with the conferences, ordering food for the seminars. But I was also doing the workload allocation model, which probably should have been the head of department's job, but that was a baptism of fire and then they didn't really know how to do it. But fine. That's learned helplessness, absolutely.

Collaboration

In your working life, you might hear reference to 'working in silos'. The academic-professional and faculty-centre divisions combined with the top-down hierarchies of many HEIs can lead to compartmentalised working. For example, there might be marketing colleagues in each faculty, the research school and the international recruitment team, as well as a centralised marketing team. Joined-up working can be tricky. Collaboration requires active effort to work across some of those social and structural boundaries.

Focusing on evidence and impact is Peter's strategy to enable better collaboration between academic and professional services colleagues:

I think collaboration is challenging because – I'm generalising horribly here – the majority of academics in universities do tend to be very driven, can see exactly what they want to do, and they can't see why nobody else wants that as well. So you've got a group of people who are excellent at their job but fail to realise that there's a bigger picture. A classic example is somebody who wants to run a specialist course because they have done a fantastic amount of research in that area and are a renowned expert. They don't see why they might not get 200 students to enrol, and I have to say to them there might be 200 people, but you have to prove that there's 200 people before we can actually run the course.

In professional services I tend to find people are, again, excellent in their own area. For example, induction might be organised separately for home and international students, but the two teams are in little silos. The challenge is to put them together and say, look, you are both right, but actually we need to find a unified approach.

> So what you've got is the driven, self-centred academics on one side, and the expert siloed professional services people on the other, and it's about trying to put them all together. I think the key thing is to just keep asking about evidence and evidence of impact. And that's the only way in which you can get people to work together.

Relationships dictate practice and engagement as much as structures in higher education. Alliances between colleagues, within and across academic and professional boundaries, and the creation of informal networks, are the means to effectively navigate the complex, changing environment and get things done. Simon observes:

> Universities are made up of so many micro-communities.

David F. sees his professional network as central to his work life:

> Networking is really important. There are people that can help you, that can back you up in a situation, all of those things. And it's really important to have those people that you value on side and to work with them and to learn from each other.

Students don't see it the same way

While we might see and experience some divisions, tensions, or disconnects between different departments or between academics and professional staff, it is important to remember that students don't have the same perspective. A student doesn't understand why there are gaps between service provision or why different parts of the HEI are not joined up. To serve students best and give the best impression and representation of our institutions, as staff members we have a duty to do the work in joined up ways, so students don't see the joins or cracks. Peter shares a very acute example:

> For me, the university is a community, and it doesn't matter who you are, you are part of that community. Students don't know everybody's role. We're doing a lot on mental health training. I am insisting we all need to be trained on this because the student won't know who they're approaching. If they're having a problem they might go and see one of the cleaners and the cleaner might be the first to be able to spot that there's a problem for a student. We can't just train personal tutors; we need to train everybody.

Digging deeper

How do historical developments (polytechnics, fees, internationalisation) continue to impact the current landscape?

Do acronyms and historic role titles hinder effective communication and inclusivity? What alternatives could be used?

How can collaboration be fostered between academics and professional services teams?

Read: Willetts, D., 2017. *A university education*. Oxford: Oxford University Press. David Willetts served as Universities Minister from 2010 to 2014. In the book he traces history, draws global comparisons, advocates for expansion, and tackles tough issues like fees and access. The book also explores future challenges like technology and globalisation, offering an in-depth look at the UK's universities in today's landscape.

Bookmark: Higher Education Acronyms, Initialisms & Abbreviations: www.hesa.ac.uk/support/definitions/acronyms.

Listen: 'Job Shadowing HE: the podcast' takes a deep dive into the roles of people who work in higher education. Featuring guests from across the sector, each episode reveals what's involved in a specific role, the career path that led to it, and tips on how to get in and get on in these jobs.

References

Barnett, R. and Di Napoli, R. eds., 2008. *Changing identities in higher education: voicing perspectives*. Abingdon, Oxon: Routledge.

Bolton, P., 2024. Research Briefing 7867: Higher Education Student Numbers. *House of Commons Library*, 2 January. Available at: <https://researchbriefings.files.parliament.uk/documents/CBP-7857/CBP-7857.pdf>.

Brown, L., 2024. National Student Accommodation Survey 2024 – Results. *Save the Student!*, 7 February. Available at: <https://www.savethestudent.org/money/surveys/national-student-accommodation-survey-2024.html>.

Caldwell, J., 2024. Nomenclature in higher education: "non-academic" as a construct. *Journal of Higher Education Policy and Management*. https://doi.org/10.1080/1360080X.2024.2306569.

Competition and Markets Authority (CMA), 2023. UK higher education providers – advice on consumer protection law. *CMA*, 31 May. Available at: <https://assets.publishing.service.gov.uk/media/64771faeb32b9e0012a95f30/Consumer_law_advice_for_higher_education_providers_.pdf>.

HESA, 2023. Staff record 2023/24 - coverage of the record. *HESA*, 8 November. Available at: <https://www.hesa.ac.uk/collection/c23025/coverage>.

HESA, 2024. Who's working in HE? *HESA*, 30 January. Available at: <https://www.hesa.ac.uk/data-and-analysis/staff/working-in-he>.

Hobson, J., Knuiman, S., Haaxman, A. and Foster, J., 2018. Building a successful partnership between professional staff and academics to improve student employability. In: C. Bossu and N. Brown, eds. 2018. *Professional and support staff in higher education*. Singapore: Springer. pp. 1–14. https://doi.org/10.1007/978-981-10-6858-4_26.

Hubbard, K., O'Neill, M. and Nattrass, S., 2021. Levelling the playing field: the effect of including widening participation in university league tables. *International Review of Education*, 67, pp. 273–304. https://doi.org/10.1007/s11159-020-09864-9.

Hughes, G. and Spanner, L., 2019. *The university mental health charter.* Leeds: Student Minds. Available at: <https://hub.studentminds.org.uk/university-mental-health-charter/>.

Khandekar, S., 2023. The lifelong loan entitlement continues to ignore online provision. *Wonkhe*, 5 July. Available at: <https://wonkhe.com/blogs/the-lifelong-loan-entitlement-continues-to-ignore-online-provision/>.

Lazell, K., 2024. What are university mission groups? *Complete University Guide*, 9 January. Available at: <www.thecompleteuniversityguide.co.uk/student-advice/where-to-study/what-are-university-mission-groups>.

Melling, L., 2019. What's in a name? Job title and working identity in professional services staff in higher education. *Perspectives: Policy and Practice in Higher Education*, 23(2–3), pp. 48–53. https://doi.org/10.1080/13603108.2018.1535459.

Office for Students (OfS), 2022. Regulatory framework. *OfS*, 24 November. Available at: <www.officeforstudents.org.uk/media/1231efe3-e050-47b2-8e63-c6d99d95144f/regulatory_framework_2022.pdf>.

Office for Students (OfS), 2023a. About the teaching excellence framework. *OfS*, 28 September. Available at: <www.officeforstudents.org.uk/advice-and-guidance/the-tef/about-the-tef>.

Office for Students (OfS), 2023b. Regulatory notice 1: access and participation plan guidance. *OfS*, 7 December. Available at: <https://www.officeforstudents.org.uk/publications/regulatory-notice-1-access-and-participation-plan-guidance/>.

Quality Assurance Agency (QAA), 2023. UK quality code for higher education. *QAA*, 10 May. Available at: <www.qaa.ac.uk/docs/qaa/quality-code/revised-uk-quality-code-for-higher-education.pdf>.

Quality Assurance Agency (QAA), 2024. Subject benchmark statements. *QAA*, March. Available at: <www.qaa.ac.uk/the-quality-code/subject-benchmark-statements>.

Research Excellent Framework (REF), 2024. What is the REF?. *REF*. Available at: <https://www.ref.ac.uk/about/what-is-the-ref/>.

Universities Scotland, 2024. Working to widen access. *Universities Scotland*. Available at: <www.universities-scotland.ac.uk/publications/working-to-widen-access/>.

Universities UK (UUK), 2024. Introducing UUK. *UUK*. Available at: <www.universitiesuk.ac.uk/about-us/introducing-uuk>.

Whitchurch, C., 2008. Shifting identities and blurring boundaries: the emergence of third space professionals in UK higher education. *Higher Education Quarterly*, 62(4), pp. 377–396. https://doi.org/10.1111/j.1468-2273.2008.00387.x.

White, S., White, S. and Borthwick, K., 2021. Blended professionals, technology and online learning: identifying a socio-technical third space in higher education. *Higher Education Quarterly*, 75(1), pp. 161–174. Available at: <https://doi.org/10.1111/hequ.12252>.

Chapter 2

Planning, progress, proficiency

Navigating and succeeding in professional services

Starting work in higher education administration can feel like entering a strange alternate universe full of complicated unwritten rules. From complex policies to unintuitive or contradictory regulations, the system can be frustratingly opaque. The trick to thriving in this environment is adaptability.

This chapter empowers you to create a personalised development plan to track your progress and build confidence. It emphasises the importance of honing essential skills like communication, leadership, and problem-solving. Career paths in this dynamic field are rarely linear. Members of our community of practice share their inspiring stories and offering valuable tips on building credibility and confidence.

A job or a career?

Not everyone wants to engage in 'building a career' or 'moving up the ladder'. If that is you, does that mean this book has little to offer you? Absolutely not. Change is constant in higher education. Our roles are continuously evolving. We are always learning and moving forward in our own professional development. Career progression is your journey to reach your full professional potential. It's not just about climbing the ladder; it's finding meaning and fulfilment in your work. It's about continuous growth, exploration, and maximising your impact as David D. explains:

> When we talk about development, it doesn't necessarily need to be jumping up grades, progressing to different roles. If you love this job, let's give you as much ownership of it as possible. Let's make you feel as central and in control and valued as possible, and that's just as valid.

Every job role in the UK public sector is defined and given a salary grading according to a standardised job evaluation scheme. In higher education, we have HERA (Higher Education Role Analysis). HERA is a system designed to evaluate roles in a transparent and objective way. Think of it as a sophisticated tool that analyses each job based on crucial factors like the level of responsibility involved, the required knowledge and skills, and the contribution it makes to the HEI's success. By examining these factors through a series of questions and then assigning points based on a defined scoring system, HERA assigns each job a relative value. This value, in turn, determines the job's placement on the HEI's pay scale, ensuring fairness and consistency in how different roles are compensated. Ultimately, HERA aims to remove any subjectivity or ambiguity from the process, guaranteeing that everyone performing similar work, regardless of their specific title, receives equal pay for equal effort. It is deployed across the sector relatively consistently.

'Progression' in the sense it is most often used, as an indicator of movement up the hierarchy and pay scale, inevitably comes from changing your role and taking risks. The structure of the public sector, of which higher education is part (apart from a few exceptions), means that you will most likely need to move jobs to gain experience or move up in the organisational hierarchy. We also move from specialist to generalist (in terms of knowledge) as we become more senior, so experience at a junior level in different areas serves you well as you move into management. Movement, change, and risk will always be factors you will need to contend with.

After two years in my first job at a university, I applied for and secured a job in a different team a pay grade lower than that of my first role. Many colleagues, including my managers, told me it was a stupid decision. But it was a decision that I was completely confident in. I hadn't been happy in my previous role. I had identified my skills gaps. I felt that I had struggled with the role because I didn't have the foundational understanding of the student administrative and learning journey that it relied on and that I would gain in my new role as a course administrator.

For me, it was absolutely the right decision. In the new role, I was fortunate to work with some super knowledgeable administrators in a kind, empowered, confident team. I learnt a huge amount of technical knowledge and worked with a diverse group of academic and support staff. I had fun. I made some wonderful friends. It was a moment in time where some superb opportunities and people came together to benefit me. The generosity of spirit – sharing knowledge, expertise, opportunity, and privileges – that I benefited from is something I have since embedded in my own professional practice. There shall be no gatekeeping of knowledge or wisdom on my watch!

I don't share this to suggest that this is specifically something you might need to do, but to reinforce that progression in your career is self-defined. It's your career. You are not on a pathway; you are forging your own path.

No two career paths are the same

There is no average career path or route in higher education professional services. Within teams or specialisms, such as HR, finance, IT, or student support, there are opportunities to progress up pay grades through the internal hierarchy. For example, Admissions Assistant to Admissions Officer to Admissions Manager. But increasingly those routes are limited, not least by the fact we all have to work much longer. There are fewer opportunities at each pay grade within a specialism or team due to the structure of HEIs. Neither I, nor any of the contributors to this book, followed a linear path in their career. Here are some of their stories. All of which illustrate unique twists and turns! Their journeys illustrate that we are not bound by our previous roles, but with a focus on our skills and experiences, there are more opportunities available to us than we might initially think.

David D. finished his A-levels and started a band. Somehow, he went from musician to Head of Operations at a large, established Russell Group university:

> I sang in a band, but I needed to pay the bills, so I got a job in a bookshop and worked in retail for a couple of years before getting my first office job in a housing association. I then moved on to work in a defunct organisation called the Legal Complaints Service, which was investigating complaints about solicitors. I started as admin there and then became a complaint handling case worker. When that place closed down, I wanted to find a role that was more local and was happy to take a bit of a pay cut because I wouldn't be commuting. So I ended up working in an admin role at one of the big accountancy firms, which didn't really gel with my values and what I wanted from the workplace. I wanted somewhere to work where I could be a little bit myself and which was not too micromanaging and formal and corporate.
>
> I applied to the University of Birmingham, Aston and BCU, probably about 20 times before I got an interview, and was delighted to get an interview here [University of Birmingham] for the first job entry-level admin job that I had. I think that was a great introduction to the world of higher education for me.
>
> Our business school restructured, as they always do, and I became academic support team leader. So I'd been here a year and three months, and that time was spent taking four department administrators and turning them into a school team. That was my first line management gig. I was the youngest person in the team by 20 plus years and the only chap.
>
> Later, when a secondment opportunity came up in our registry team I was delighted to get it. Pretty quickly a couple of members of the team left and I was able to secure a permanent role in the team at the grade above my old job.
>
> After four and a half years, I was ready to bounce, and I wanted to line manage again. So I thought, well, what have I not done? Research support. This job came up, starting a team from scratch, and I thought, well, hey, why not do that? And it was a sideways move. I then made another sideways move into operations before I moved up into my current role.

Simon wanted to get some administration experience after having worked as a teacher for four years. He has never looked back:

> I started at the University of Salford as a temp and my first job was sorting out a physics professor's filing system. Although the work wasn't particularly stimulating, I could see that working at the university had the potential to be really fulfilling. The university then, and still is, a really friendly place to work, so it was a real moment. It reminds me of those 'choose your own adventure' books: I can choose this path and where will that lead? Or I can go back to the safety and security of teaching. So I just took a gamble. And that was 23 years ago.

Sarah came to higher education 'by accident' (her words) on a temporary contract, after working for many years in marketing in the financial services sector:

> The variety keeps me interested. No two days are the same. No two years are the same. And the challenge is always there.

Jenny had no idea that working in a university was an option:

> I went to university, but school had made that happen. My mum couldn't believe that I actually went to university. When I finished, I didn't know what I was going to do so I went to Spain for six months. When I came back, one of my best friends had a job in a factory doing admin, accounts, cleaning, everything. She was leaving, so I said, 'I'll have your job'. That was how career driven I was!
>
> So she told her boss that's what I was going to do, and I worked in this awful job for a year thinking: 'What am I doing? Why am I doing this?' And then I saw an advert in the paper for a Student Support Assistant. I had never been so excited about a job. I worked really hard on my application, and I really wanted that job. I just was so excited to think, 'I've just been to uni and now I could have a job helping students and I'm only just out of it.'
>
> I got the job, and I absolutely loved it. It was just brilliant. I loved working with the students and the academics, and it felt like a serious job. I can remember taking the academic regulations home to read, to learn, because I wanted to know what I was talking about. I wanted to be good. I wanted people to think I was good. I wanted to know it all. I wanted to soak it all up.

Mehmet used his background in data analytics as a springboard to define his own journey through higher education. After graduating he completed a six-month internship as a data analyst at a university:

> The internship opened up my eyes. I saw behind the scenes in higher education. As it was only for about six months, I quickly realised that

I needed to figure out something more permanent. The next pivotal moment was taking up a permanent position in admissions, which is how I got involved in student recruitment. It was quite different to my initial few months at the university, going from hardcore analytics and strategic initiatives to processing – the student and customer facing work and activities. I don't think I'd have got that role if it wasn't for my initial experience. I'm 80 per cent sure of that. But what I'm 100 per cent sure of is, I wouldn't have known that role even existed, and I wouldn't have been able to go down this path at all, had it not been for my initial entry through the internship.

My first permanent role was an admin-heavy one where I was literally requesting references for 35 hours a week from postgraduate students, in very manual ways!. My colleagues and wider team recognised that things could have been done differently in this area, but they didn't have the right kind of support or resource or skills to make that change themselves as an admissions team. But with my more technical background, I sensed the opportunity to innovate and create meaningful, impactful changes. I never let that go. I thought about what the next five years looks like and I set myself the target of trying to become a head of service.

Even though there wasn't much in the way of reporting or anything like that at that time, I made sure it became part of that role and I made sure to lean into that space and provide my expertise, to play into my strengths. And it wasn't a lot of expertise back then, to be honest, but it was definitely something that I think others appreciated, or there was a need for, and it made lives easier for others. I that's the foundation that I built my early career on, leaning as much as possible into data, working as closely as possible with senior colleagues.

David F. didn't know what he wanted to do when he first graduated:

I fell into a job in a letting agency. I rented a house with some friends to figure out what I wanted to do, and they offered me a job. It was all a bit random. I ended up staying there for four years. I learned a lot about meeting people and getting to grips with the communication side of things, which certainly didn't come naturally to me at that stage. Then I moved into a recruitment role for a year, which I hated. I just wasn't invested in it.

That's when I started to have a real shift in terms of feeling I needed to care about what I was doing, otherwise I was just going to disengage. To begin with, it was more about how I could utilise a skill set that I'd built up, and that was web and graphic design. I'd always loved media studies and writing and that kind of thing, what role is that? Oh, it's marketing!

My first move into marketing was with a provider of educational workshops to schools. I got to do all the hands-on stuff that you might imagine comes with marketing – video production, website, copywriting, design – all of those elements weaved together, and it was really interesting. But I very quickly realised my career wasn't going to be there. There was nowhere to grow. Even though it wasn't education per se, it was kind of supporting education and that's what made me look at the HE sector and think, I can get on board with this, because I believe in what they're doing. My first role was being the marketing person for the university library.

These stories demonstrate that careers are not straightforward, and 'progression' takes many forms. There can be pressure to 'progress'. Progression tends to be talked about in a slightly heavy way, referred to in terms of an upwards movement, as if it were a Victorian march towards enlightenment and authority. But that isn't how most careers turn out, especially in higher education. Career paths are not linear anymore. You can define your own progression and development. Sarah offers her take on this:

> There's such a difference between having a job and a career, but there's also quite a nice space in the middle where people really want to do a good job without actively seeking promotion: they're interested in enjoying what they do and doing it well.

Don't be rigid about your long-term career plan or what you feel you ought to be doing. Be open to opportunities that might suit you even if they don't seem to fit with your current plan. Very few people follow the career path they intend or expect to.

Getting started

If you have just joined higher education, where is the best place to start learning the ropes? First, get reading! HEIs produce lots of policies, procedures, strategies, regulations, papers, and much more.

Find information

Start by reading the organisation's official documentation. This could include handbooks, policies, regulations, and online resources. Everything you need should be available on your institution's intranet. These documents hold the key to understanding your institution's systems, structures, procedures, and expectations. You may also want to learn about the external bodies that impact your work. The more you know – or, at least, the more you know where to find things – the less daunting the path ahead will appear. Sarah reassures:

> As long as you work within those fixed parameters, you can't go too wrong because you've got that anchor of what is actually right.

But regulations, policies, processes, and systems, do change, and they change often. So do not save any documents to your computer– always go to the current online version. Bookmark the relevant links in your internet browser.

Network

Getting to know people in your team and in teams with which you will need to collaborate is important. Try to build relationships with colleagues including people from different departments and levels of seniority. Their insights and guidance can be invaluable, as Sarah explains:

> Get yourself a peer group. Talk to people elsewhere in the university at your level. Find a group of people on whom you can rely, bounce ideas off, ask advice without feeling like they are going to think, 'Why don't you know that?'

Diverse relationships broaden your network, expose you to fresh perspectives, and open doors to opportunities. David D. finds it stimulating to engage with others:

> I've always been energised by spending time with people, and I think that's one of the things that's kept me here for so long. And AHEP [Association of Higher Education Professionals] has been great because it's built my network across the sector. I do trade on the network, and I do take a lot of joy and energy from it.

Ask questions

Asking questions is a sign of initiative and a vital part of the learning journey. Seek clarification, context, and practical advice from your managers and experienced colleagues. It's equally important to have strategies to record/retain information. It's okay to ask the same question once or twice, but exasperation will build if you ask the same question too many times!

Do verify any process or policy information you are told verbally. A re-occurring example from my career relates to students wanting to return to the university after having been exited. Course administrators I have worked with for years, both when I was a course administrator and then in admissions, would say with absolute certainty: 'A student cannot go back onto a course that they've failed.' It became common lore. It was undisputed. However, it had never been in the regulations. It was a misunderstanding of a regulation about permitting a unit to be retaken a limited number of times. Yet, I had colleagues tell me repeatedly that returning was not permitted. I would ask them to show me the regulation where this was stated so I could demonstrate that they were incorrect. Perhaps it had been in the regulations at some point in the past. People do have long memories!

Learn the unwritten rules

While policies and procedures provide a framework within which we work, success in any organisation requires an understanding of its unwritten culture.

This unwritten lore is the currency of influence, the ability to understand and navigate the hidden norms, values, and expectations that shape the environment. Observe. Watch how senior leaders and colleagues conduct themselves and interact. Pay attention to their communication styles, and how they navigate different situations. Alongside what you learn from your colleagues, you'll start to decode the institution's cultural code and gain a deeper understanding of how things truly work.

Be open-minded

Try not to let pre-existing expectations or assumptions influence your judgment. Being receptive to new ideas, even if they challenge your own beliefs, is valuable. However, do critically engage with information and validate it for yourself. Don't just accept everything you hear. Think critically and check information for yourself. Remember, everyone has their own point of view, and no one is completely unbiased. A lot of people will share their perspectives with you and it's best to remember that no narrator is impartial. By being open and critical (in the sense of verifying information or challenging strong views), you'll understand things better and navigate situations more easily.

Developing skills and knowledge

I asked everyone who contributed their voice to this book what skills they think are foundational for succeeding in professional services. Three themes emerged: communication, problem-solving, and a strategic view.

Communication

Effective communication is paramount, but it is not straightforward. It involves actively listening, expressing yourself clearly, and adapting your communication style to your audience. It is about sharing information and being open and honest, and checking for understanding to avoid misunderstandings. In all of your communications, you need to consider your audience, purpose, and context. Effective communication happens when you think before you speak or send an email or message. Remember to invest time and energy into building strong relationships.

Embedded within the concept of effective communication are the skills of tact and diplomacy. These skills are vital when you are communicating. Remember, it's not just what you say, but it's how you say it and how well you engage with what you hear as you listen, that matters.

Beyond communicating outwardly and actively listening, you are also facilitating the communication of others. Loud voices can drown out quieter ones. Make space and invite others to contribute.

Sarah continues to marvel at how difficult clear communication can be:

> I never, ever stop being amazed by what people hear when you communicate. You cannot communicate enough, and people still hear something different. I've thought that my entire career and I've never resolved it. You think you've said something, or you've written something very clearly, people then interpret it in a totally different way, and they can build a perception of something that isn't true.

An example of miscommunication for me happened while working with a government department on the pilot for a new teacher training admissions application system for England and Wales. The system had already been built and tested with a smaller group of specialist providers. Members of my admissions team and I met with the project team on a fortnightly basis. We explained in detail the challenges and requirements for the system based on our experience of the market, applicant pool, compliance requirements, and other factors. Six months into working closely with the project team, I suddenly realised that my colleagues and I were working to a completely different definition of the term 'international applicant' than the project team from the government department.

It dawned on me that the project team was working on the basis that an 'international applicant' was someone who had not completed their high school studies in the UK. This meant their definition included many people who are UK nationals or settled in the UK and who are not international applicants by any higher education definition. I explained that I had assumed everyone was working to the definition embedded in legislation (fee assessment regulations). The response I got was, 'That might be *your* definition, but for the purposes of this project this is the definition we are using.' I pointed out it wasn't *my* definition, but *their* government's definition. They weren't impressed.

This experience taught me never, ever to assume a shared understanding – even if it seems obvious. More specifically definitions often go undefined in higher education, which can be a challenge. It is always worth establishing them at the start of a project or conversation and refer to any external benchmarks (for example, the Quality Assurance Agency or legislation) for starting points in specifying definitions.

Communication between academic and professional colleagues, or between departments is a common occurrence. I have always working with a student records system that names each data view and processing function with a three-letter code, such as SPD, MAV, and ATR. Many a professional services team member has confounded an academic or senior leader referring to 'ATR-ing' an applicant. Better to refer to 'ATR-ing' as transferring an applicant to the enrolment stage once all the relevant conditions have been met. That will probably make more sense to them!

Problem-solving

Problem-solving encompasses skills of creativity and originality, critical thinking, analysis, reasoning, and adaptability. It's particularly key in higher education as a sector that is subject to multiple conflicting influences, continuous change, and multiple different personalities. Solving problems effectively, diplomatically, and pragmatically is the primary way that those not in academic roles can build credibility (instead of academic credentials and number of publications) (Coate, Kandiko Howson & Yu Yang, 2018).

David F. shares an example of putting this skill into practice:

> I remember my manager would regularly come in and say, 'I'm off to a meeting in a minute, can you give me all the figures?' And I would think to myself, 'I'm in the middle of something. I wish you'd give me some warning.' That's what forced me to learn to use a digital tool for all the web analytics reports so when they suddenly ask for data, I can just send them a link and it's got everything on it in a dynamic report. I don't have to scrabble around and do all of that stuff each time someone asks.

A strategic view

It is vital that you understand how your role and your work fit into the bigger picture, which can be articulated as the ability to take a strategic view. You need to consider the needs of the organisation as a commercial enterprise and not just an educational and/or administrative body. We all must be operational, fulfilling day-to-day tasks and short-term goals. Take a strategic view means stepping back and considering longer term aims, wider context, and the needs of the whole organisation. The trick here is finding the right balance.

Mehmet explains how he puts this into practice:

> I feel that the operational is sometimes missing from the strategic and sometimes the strategic is missing from the operational. That little bit of context about the other side goes a long way.
>
> I think the most important balance is to get the operational teams thinking about things strategically. I think the way to achieve this is to try to align the activities that the operational teams are doing to something tangible. So in my case, that is our subject strategy or corporate strategy, that is, where are we trying to grow? What are the most important strands of activity for student recruitment?
>
> All universities, modern universities especially, try to do a lot of things. There's lots and lots of ways for things to fly. And of those, something has got to be important, and something has got to be slightly less important. There's got to be a sense at the institution of what they want to achieve or

which direction they wish to go. This is where the strategic people come into play. They have to have that direction of travel. They have to have that recognition and acknowledgment of what they want the institution size and shape to be. And that's the bit that you take to the operational teams and say, 'We need to work and align our activities in relation to this.' If everything works as it should, those are the kind of things that people will often ask questions about, or report on, or monitor at the institution. It might be through KPIs [key performance indicators], it might be through local delivery plans, or more specific targets.

For a well-functioning organisation, everything that the organisation does, should be aligned to those things at a strategic level. And so when it comes to setting that work, thinking about what initiatives and what activities to put in place, it should mirror that.

Assessing your skills and competencies

Your job description tells you the **purpose** of your role and **tasks** you need to complete. The person specification outlines the **knowledge** and **skills** required to do the job. These elements are central to focusing your approach on professional development. But what skills do you need to focus on developing further (whether that is in your current role or beyond)?

There are many tools available that can help us assess our skills and abilities. AHEP has developed a framework of eight professional competencies for those working in higher education administration. Each is accompanied by a description and examples of behaviours that reflect positive impact. It can be found on the AHEP website (link in the Digging Deeper section of this chapter). Sarah finds it a helpful tool for assessing current performance and identifying areas of focus for professional development and career planning:

> The AHEP competency framework is about having the whole package. It's all the things you need to do.

To use this tool, start with what you are already doing. Use the descriptors to assess your current confidence in each of the areas.

As a guide, let's work through how you might approach one of the AHEP (2023) commitments: 'Working Together'. This commitment focuses on collaboration and communication. Confidence communicating and collaborating with a wide range of stakeholders (students, parents, academics, professional bodies, employers, recruitment agents) is important. Sarah highlights the value of this skill:

> Administrators talk to each other. You know, the academics will ask, 'How do you know this?' The answer is, 'Because we communicate!' But that is

our strength. It's essential that we know what other people are doing so that we can come to solutions together.

Ask yourself: what do I do well in this area? What could I do better? Am I comfortable using email but get nervous on the phone? How do I approach teamwork? Do I avoid group projects?

I always found working collaboratively challenging. I managed to avoid group work throughout my entire degree study. I was used to having my own workload that I could manage independently. Then I became a course administrator, and I had shared responsibility for a portfolio of courses with another colleague on a different campus. This was before we had Microsoft Teams as a way to communicate face to face. We had telephones, email and an extremely basic online chat tool (which was not as advanced as MSN Messenger, if you remember those days).

I think my colleague and I drove our manager to distraction with our repeated complaints about each other. 'They are always checking up on me and expecting me to make mistakes,' I'd protest. 'They don't trust me to do my job.' I knew I was being thorough and doing a good job. I could not fathom why my colleague was always checking my work and telling me what to do. After some frustrating weeks, I had a long, hard think about what I could do to form a more positive working relationship with this colleague. I spoke with my manager and my colleague. I came to understand that my colleague was cautious about trusting me based on previous experiences of having to correct work or pick up work others had not completed. This person didn't know me. They weren't to know I could be trusted to complete my tasks to an appropriate standard and meet our shared deadlines.

After this realisation, I reframed my approach. Instead of getting frustrated and complaining, I set myself a mission to prove myself to my colleague. I'm competitive (as were they) so it became a game. I was determined to have every task completed just ahead of schedule so that when they asked me about it, it would already have been completed. Through this experience, I identified that sometimes we need to demonstrate our skills and competencies to others to facilitate a positive collaboration – we can't expect people to trust us from the start. A reputation is earned, regardless of previous experience in another role or organisation.

My change of approach worked. Soon enough we were working so well together that we became annoying to our manager in an entirely new way! We collaborated so effectively that we were able to identify an issue, ask our manager about it, discuss it while we wait for our manager to consider it, find the solution, and resolve it, before our manager even had the time to look at the problem.

Be honest with yourself regarding your current level of competence and confidence assessing yourself against, for example, the AHEP framework. Keep a record so you can reflect back in the future and see the progress you have made.

IT skills and keeping up with digital technologies

A common thread running through the skills of communication, problem-solving, and thinking strategically, is IT literacy. In an increasingly digital world, our ability to utilise technology effectively goes beyond everyday smartphone use. From crafting presentations to deciphering online information, a robust set of digital skills has become necessary at work. Employers are actively seeking individuals who can communicate clearly, innovate using technology, and navigate the ever-evolving digital landscape. However, in this area, self-reflection is key. Can you critically assess information found online? Do you choose the most appropriate tool for the task at hand? Are you managing your digital identities in a way that aligns with your values and those of your employer?

Actively exploring and developing digital skills in areas like information literacy, data analysis, creative problem-solving, and time management are crucial to success in this digital age. By taking control of your digital capabilities, you empower yourself to confidently navigate the opportunities and challenges of a world increasingly shaped by technology and support an economically sustainable future.

Jisc (2024) has developed a framework of digital capabilities to 'equip someone to live, learn and work in a digital society'. Alongside the framework are customised role profiles for those working in higher education and further education as researchers, teachers, learning technologists, students, learning resources staff, and professional services staff. Use it to help you set goals for yourself.

Setting goals

Having defined the knowledge, skills and behaviours you want to focus on developing, the next step is to create an action plan. In this context it's usually referred to as a Professional Development Plan (PDP). This is simply an actionable plan in which you record your goals, monitor progress and define your accomplishments.

You may be asked do this exercise as part of your annual appraisal. In terms of your professional development, ultimately no one will do it for you. Your annual appraisal is likely to be focused primarily on your current role and targets based on strategic direction. For your own personal PDP, find a template that suits your style (there are many available freely on the internet). Remember, this is your plan, not your employer's, so find the best template for you and try to find a balance between your immediate development needs and your longer-term aspirations. Simon reminds us:

> We're at work so much of our life. It has to give you a reward in some way, and you have to decide what your rewards are, what the rewards are for you, and what you need to get out of that.

Ensuring your goals are attainable

Goals without deadlines are just aspirations. Your goals need to be achievable within a reasonable timeframe without adding extra stress to your life. I recommend using the SMART structure. You may have been asked to set SMART objectives as part of your induction or annual review process. SMART stands for Specific, Measurable, Achievable, Relevant and Timely. It sounds straightforward in principle, but in practice it can be hard to apply. Most people struggle with SMART objectives, particularly the measurable part. Here is some guidance on putting the principles into practice.

1 **Specificity**: What exactly do you want to achieve? Action verbs like 'analyse', 'create', 'identify' or 'implement' are your friends here.
2 **Measurability**: Instead of 'reduce data errors' aim for 'reduce data errors by 25 per cent by [date]'. Alternatively, define completion by clear progress point, such as 'submit the proposal to the committee by [date]'.
3 **Achievability**: It's good to stretch yourself, but setting an impossible target just leads to discouragement or sets you up to fail. What will you need to achieve your goal? What help might you need from others? Remember, flexibility is crucial – adjust resources and approach as needed to stay on track. Include long- and short-term goals.
4 **Relevance**: Align your objectives with your role and the bigger picture. HEIs publish their values and their strategic plan on their website. You can align your goals for your annual review/induction to these. However, for your own PDP, you might wish to consider your own values and those of any professional body that is relevant to your area of work. (For example, as I work in admissions, my professional goals relating to my admissions work always relate to the Universities UK Code of Practice for Fair Admissions (UUK, 2023).)
5 **Timeliness**: Deadlines are motivators and keep us accountable. Set clear time frames, with smaller milestones along the way, to keep you focused and avoid last-minute scrambles. Think of them as building blocks to success.

That's the theory. Here is an example in practice:

What is the goal? By 31 July, increase the self-service rate for obtaining course enrolment letters by 20 per cent among undergraduate students compared to the previous academic year.
How will it be measured? Track the number of enrolment letters downloaded through the online portal compared to the number requested via in-person or email communication.
How will it be achieved? On the online portal for obtaining enrolment letters, guidance will be simplified, and step-by-step visuals added. The availability

of self-service options will be communicated through multiple channels, including student inductions, departmental forums, and social media. Feedback will be gathered from students on their experience with self-service enrolment letter download and the insights will be used to continuously improve the process.

What will the impact be? Increased self-service adoption saves students time and reduces administrative workload, leading to a more efficient and accessible service experience. Improved ease of use fosters student satisfaction and reduces frustration with administrative processes.

SMART objectives offer a framework for success and should not feel restrictive. Embrace flexibility, adjust as needed, and celebrate your progress as you achieve your milestones.

Professional development takes many forms

When considering how to achieve your goals and develop your professional skills, training is not the only solution. Professional development is not the same as training. Training is one aspect of professional development. This misconception sometimes frustrates Sarah:

> One of the things people need to understand is that CPD [Continuing Professional Development] is not training. CPD comes from so many other activities, and you are developing skills and competencies in lots of ways besides formal training. Staff tell me they want training and I think, 'No, you don't, what you want is development, and development comes in lots of different ways.'

David F. describe learning and development as a means to create space for innovation and exploration:

> You have to generate your own learning experiences to some degree so get all the core stuff done that you know needs to be done and out of the door. To do it well, get it down how you need to deliver it. And then if you've got room, you have that room to play, to experiment, to develop, and that fills up your tank.

By job shadowing you can observe colleagues in new roles, gleaning insights and skills beyond your own. Jenny feels it should be promoted more:

> I think working across boundaries and shadowing other teams is really important and it's not something that happens enough. We need to encourage more of that, don't we? Working in different departments and a bit of job shadowing.

Supporting organisation-wide activity, such as graduation and open days, offers valuable experience and fresh perspectives. (There's usually an element of waiting about on graduation days and this provides a perfect opportunity for networking as you can chat with colleagues from different teams while you wait.) Volunteering to be involved with projects (from role-specific to staff networks) offers opportunities to develop relationships with peers for knowledge exchange and collaboration. Self-directed learning through online courses, podcasts and industry publications keeps you up to date on emerging issues and developments.

Recording accomplishments

Track everything you achieve in terms of professional development, from successfully navigating a tense meeting to mastering a new piece of software. This documentation is for you, and no one will judge whether something ought to be included. An achievement, such as a tweak to a process, might seem small, but in time, bigger consequences and benefits may come that you'll be able to track back to that initial change you made.

Seeing your achievements laid out before you helps build confidence and empowers you to reach for higher goals. When opportunities for projects or a new role arise, you'll have concrete evidence of your contributions. Self-doubt and imposter syndrome can be tempered on bad days by reviewing your achievements. Julie found it a powerful technique:

> I've encouraged people to step off the treadmill, so to speak, and take time to document their skills and achievements and experience, because once they do that and they start committing it to paper, they'll be surprised at the breadth of what they deal with. Normally they take so much of it for granted. So taking some time to step back is really important. And if you can get a trusted colleague that can review it with you, that's even more powerful. Because then they can start to push you on elements where you're perhaps too modest.

Here are some ideas to get you started:

- **Quantitative wins:** reaching financial goals, exceeding project targets, improving metrics.
- **Qualitative wins**: resolving conflicts, mastering new skills, exceeding expectations, receiving praise or recognition (if you got that compliment in an email – keep it to revisit when you are having a more challenging day!).
- **Personal growth:** overcoming challenges, learning from mistakes, developing new skills.
- **Impact:** positive feedback from colleagues or students, contributions to team success, innovations implemented.

My achievement tracker is a simple spreadsheet with these headings:

- Date
- Project
- Project Task/Description/Issue
- My contribution
- Contribution to strategic goals
- Stakeholders
- Contribution to the stakeholders
- Key performance indicator
- Reflections

Track your victories, big and small, and celebrate your incredible professional journey. You will see that you've accomplished more than you think, and you deserve to recognise your own brilliance.

Achieving your goals

Setting goals is just the beginning of professional development. It's just as important to consider what might get in the way of your achieving your goals as thinking about the goals themselves. In higher education, we talk a lot about barriers for applicants and students. Ask yourself: what structural and mental barriers will I have to overcome to achieve my goals? Take these into account when setting them. You don't want to set yourself up for failure with a lot of challenging targets. Better to have a small number of considered and realistic goals in your plan than a number of daunting and potentially unattainable ones. If you have one or two bigger goals, perhaps break them down into smaller stages. For example, securing a promotion could be broken down into steps, such as, taking on responsibility for a big project, offering to stand in for your manager when they go on annual leave, and arranging to shadow a senior leader in their role.

Believe in yourself

We all lack confidence at times, and it can be hard to overcome. Jenny shared:

> I have absolutely no confidence in my own abilities, but my boss does, so I get asked to be involved in things which sometimes fill me with fear because I just don't think I'm good enough.

I asked her how she overcame her fear, as to many this fear might be paralysing. She explained:

> I think it's because I really do want to do a good job. I want to be well thought of. I want to make things better for people. I'm also really nosy!

I want to know about other things, I want to learn about other areas. I want to get to know people in other teams, especially at the OU [Open University] as it is so huge, so vast. I'm just so intrigued about how it all works. I think you can always make things better, make a difference, and that's really important to me. I don't want to just stagnate in a role that I can do with my eyes closed. I don't do that. There are always things that come up in a team and I'll always put myself forward for those.

You might compare yourself to others and discount your own potential, which Simon cautions against:

As long as you are always looking for the next development opportunity, you don't have to apologise for being somewhere for a long time. Same as you don't have to apologise for being somewhere for a short period of time if it wasn't right or something else came up. It's that thing of not apologising for choices that you've made. If you can justify them to yourself, then you should be comfortable with that and where you are and what you bring to an organisation. And I think that's the thing where it comes back to change. Sometimes you do outgrow a job. You've done as much as you can do in that role, and that's okay, too.

As you get more experienced and involved, you will build credibility. People will seek out your opinion and start to listen to you. Lean into your strengths and keep referring back to your achievements to remind yourself that you can do your job well, you are a valuable member of the team, and you can achieve your goals.

Digging deeper

How do the shared stories challenge traditional notions of career progression? What possibilities do they open up for your own career journey?

What resources and tools available within your institution can support your professional development?

How can you leverage informal learning opportunities, such as work-shadowing, to enrich your professional development planning?

Read: Gander, M., Moyes, H. and Sabzalieva, E., 2014. *Managing your career in higher education administration.* London: Palgrave Macmillan. (The ebook can often be accessed through your HEI's library using your staff log in.)

Visit: Association of Higher Education Professionals (AHEP): www.ahep.ac.uk/. The professional association for higher education professional services started in 1961 and was called the Association of University Administrators (AUA) until 2023. Lots of free professional development resources are available here including the AHEP Professional Framework.

Assess: National Careers Services skills health check and toolkit: https://nationalcareers.service.gov.uk/skills-assessment and https://nationalcareers.service.gov.uk/find-a-course/the-skills-toolkit.

References

Association of Higher Education Professionals (AHEP), 2023. Using the AHEP framework. *AHEP*. Available at: <https://ahep.ac.uk/wp-content/uploads/2023/10/Using-the-AHEP-Framework.pdf>.

Coate, K., Kandiko Howson, C. and Yu Yang, T., 2018. Senior professional leaders in higher education: the role of prestige final report. *Society for Research into Higher Education (SRHE)*, January. Available at: <https://srhe.ac.uk/wp-content/uploads/2020/03/Report_SRHE_CoateKandikoHowson2018.pdf>.

Jisc, 2024. Individual digital capabilities. *Jisc*. Available at: <https://digitalcapability.jisc.ac.uk/what-is-digital-capability/individual-digital-capabilities/>.

Universities UK (UUK), 2023. Fair admissions code of practice. *UUK*, 9 August. Available at: <https://www.universitiesuk.ac.uk/what-we-do/policy-and-research/publications/fair-admissions-code-practice>.

Chapter 3

Target, tailor, triumph
Mastering the job search and interview

This chapter aims to equips you with everything you need to navigate the application and interview process with confidence. It will cover the entire journey, from unearthing the perfect opportunity and demystifying the Higher Education Role Analysis (HERA) framework to crafting a compelling supporting statement that showcases your strengths. Filled with practical worked examples, this chapter tackles interview nerves and gives you the tools to help you to shine in your interactions with potential employers.

The search

Most higher education institutions (HEIs) advertise their vacant posts on their own website and on LinkedIn. Some also post to jobs.ac.uk, but not all, and particularly not for junior roles. So you will have to do a bit of searching to find institutions you would like to work for and keep an eye on their advertised jobs.

Once you've spotted one, you can review the job advert and start to prepare an application.

A bit of background

The HERA framework governs how job descriptions and person specifications are created. The **job description** shows what a role is all about, what the employee will be doing, and why it's important. But the **person specification** gets more specific – it's a checklist of what the organisation is looking for in the perfect person to fill that role. This checklist includes the skills, knowledge, qualifications, and experience the candidate needs to have to do the job really well. It's also the criteria the hiring manager will use to shortlist candidates for interview. This is crucial information to keep in mind when drafting an application. For all jobs in the UK public sector, instead of sending a CV, the candidate must carefully and systematically fill out an application form.

DOI: 10.4324/9781003522126-4

When applying for a job in higher education, don't be afraid to speak to the recruiting manager to find out more about a role. Joanne urges:

Just talk to them and say, 'I'm interested in it. Can you tell me a bit about a bit more about it?'

Your application

It is a useful exercise to put yourself in the shoes of the hiring manager. An important question you should keep in mind is: what is going to make my application stand out?

The key element of the application is the supporting statement or personal statement. This is your opportunity to showcase your suitability for the role and convince the hiring manager to invite you for an interview. Every public sector role comes with a job description and a person specification, outlining the criteria employed by hiring managers for shortlisting. If you aspire to be shortlisted, your supporting statement must unequivocally demonstrate you meet all the essential criteria, and as many of the desirable criteria as possible.

The most effective supporting statements systematically address each criterion, providing concrete examples of how the candidate possesses the necessary knowledge, skills, behaviours, and experience. Crucially, they clearly articulate how relevant experience and transferable skills can be applied to the specific job being applied for. It doesn't need lots of long words. David D suggests:

Ask yourself, 'what will make my application easiest to read?' Make it clear, as well as making it stand out.

Writing a supporting statement

I know I'm not alone in experiencing writer's block when attempting to draft a supporting statement for a job interview. Despite my enthusiasm for the position and confidence in my skills, the blank screen often paralyses me. To combat this challenge, here are three strategies that I have found effective:

1 **Dictate your thoughts:** Keep your phone handy to capture ideas as they arise, whether it's a brilliant concept, a successful project, or a valuable discussion point. This method is especially beneficial for those who struggle with written communication or find long-form writing daunting. Note-taking apps and dictation features integrated into software such as Word and Google Docs can be helpful tools.
2 **Break down the process into manageable chunks:** Don't attempt to tackle the entire supporting statement in one sitting. Instead, during the regular work week, make quick notes whenever you encounter a task that aligns

with the job requirements. For instance, if you start the day responding to student queries, jot down the aspects that relate to the person's specification, such as communicating with different audiences. This method ensures you don't overlook crucial details.
3 **Start in the middle**: While many people feel compelled to start at the beginning, I've found that starting in the middle triggers my creative flow. I gather ideas first and then refine the introduction and conclusion later. This approach aligns with my thought process and allows me to focus on the essence of my message before worrying about structure.

The key is to simply start writing. Don't overthink or get bogged down by perfection. Let your thoughts flow as you systematically work through the person specification, and the supporting statement will gradually take shape. You can tidy it up later. I like using the read-aloud tools in Word or Google Docs to help me find mistakes or improve the flow.

Evidencing your experience in your supporting statement

You will be expected to stick within a maximum word or character count, and you will want to keep your statement to the point and specific. Avoid restating the criteria or giving long descriptions of elements of your current role. The person reviewing your application wants to know exactly how you meet the criteria in the specification. They'd rather hear how you will apply your experience to the advertised role than a long narrative about responsibilities in your current role.

Here is an example set of criteria for the role of international admissions manager in an English HEI:

1 Experience of UK higher education admissions
2 Understanding of relevant legislation
3 Experience in leading, managing, and developing staff

So here your response might be: 'I have a deep understanding of current legislation'.

This doesn't tell the recruiting manager anything and suggests, by omission that, actually, you don't have much knowledge.

A better statement could be:

> I have a comprehensive understanding of the UK visa regulations relevant to student applicants and the processes involved in issuing CAS [confirmation of acceptance for studies] statements, including student visa financial maintenance requirements and ENIC [European Network of Information Centres] qualification equivalency assessments.

In this second example, the recruiting manager will be sure you know something about UK higher education admissions and legislation relating to the issuing of visas for international students from this answer (Criteria 1 and 2).

A further statement could highlight how you learn about/stay up to date with regulations: 'I monitor updates and changes to UK visa regulations by subscribing to UKVI [UK Visas and Immigration] newsletters and share important updates with colleagues'.

In this statement, you are demonstrating that you are proactive and take initiative to share knowledge.

If you haven't been a line manager before, you'll need to focus on your transferable skills. In the above example, you've already demonstrated that you take the lead on sharing knowledge, that is, 'developing staff'. Additional questions you could ask yourself are: when your department was busy last year, what did you do to ensure the temporary staff kept on task? How did you support a new member of your team most recently? How did you help the student who was doing work experience with your team?

A strong final paragraph might read:

> I have a comprehensive understanding of the UK visa regulations relevant to student applicants and the processes involved in issuing CAS statements, including student visa financial maintenance requirements and ENIC qualification equivalency assessments. I monitor updates and changes to UK visa regulations by subscribing to UKVI newsletters. I have deployed my advanced knowledge by leading training sessions on regulatory requirements for new team members. For temporary staff under my supervision, I ensure that their performance is closely monitoring to ensure regulatory compliance.

I secured my first management role in a new-to-me team over existing members of that team who had applied for the same role. Why was I successful over others who knew more about the specific work of the department? I was able to articulate my professional philosophy of leadership and demonstrate how my portfolio of skills and experience made me the ideal candidate.

Attention to detail

In my decade of experience as a recruiting manager, I've reviewed a huge number of application forms and supporting statements. Repeatedly, I've encountered common mistakes that prevent potentially qualified candidates from being shortlisted. To ensure you're not overlooked, make sure you follow the guidelines, eliminate typos, and comprehensively fill out all requested information regarding your work experience and qualifications.

Using Generative AI tools

I use Generative Artificial Intelligence (Gen AI) tools to help me with my work on a daily basis. You may wish to use them to help you draft your supporting statement. However, I caution you to use Gen AI with care. HEIs are starting to draft and publish policies on use of Gen AI that you will need to be mindful of.

Large language models (LLMs) such as Chat GPT are language tools so they can help you communicate your ideas, but they cannot create your examples for you. If you ask an LLM to draft a personal statement based on elements of the job description and person specific that you input, it will offer something that might sound clever but won't be specific enough. A hiring manager needs to understand your unique experience, skills, and potential. You also need to follow your written statement through to the interview and you can't bring Gen AI tools to the interview.

The interview

Instead of thinking of an interview as answering questions posed by the interview panel, think of it as a means to demonstrate to the panel that you are everything they are looking for and the most suitable person for the job.

The same principle you applied to drafting your supporting statement extends to the interview stage. This is where the hiring team assess candidates against the job description and person specification. To excel, provide specific examples that demonstrate how you meet all the essential and desirable criteria, establishing yourself as the ideal candidate.

Sarah always tells people when they go to an interview:

> You don't actually know what they're looking for. You don't know who else is going for this job. So you only have to make sure that you do your best. The job may or may not be for you, but you've got to get as much out of that interview as possible. You might get the job. Brilliant. But if you're not offered the job, the better you've answered the questions the better for you, and next time you'll be ready for the right job for you.

I've been on the panel for interviews that have lasted only 15 minutes, much to the surprise of the candidate. The reason? They answered the panel's questions very superficially.

Interview questions are an opportunity – your chance to demonstrate your knowledge and share examples that evidence your proficiency. You can answer a question about what good customer service means to you with a few sentences on your philosophy about good service. Alternatively, you can outline your philosophy, give an example of good service that you have given, give an example of how you address poor customer service, and what factors you might take into account when dealing with the public around communication and accessibility. You need every answer you give to be an exposition of your skills, experience, and expertise. What does this mean for you in the days before your interview? It means that preparation is vital.

'Tell me about a time when...'

One common type of question asked at an interview are behavioural questions. By asking these, the panel are trying to find out how you work and how you might apply your skills and experience to real-life situations. Common themes include teamwork, customer service, problem-solving, communication, and time management.

Based on the job description and the person specification, you should prepare an example on each of the above themes as you are likely to need them. When we are nervous, we can ramble, so here is a handy way to frame your story, which is known as the STAR (situation, task, action, result) method.

Imagine you're in an interview and you're telling a story about a time you faced a challenge. Here's what you could tell the panel:

- **SITUATION**: Set the scene. Let them know where you were, what was happening, and why it mattered.
- **TASK**: What were you responsible for in that situation? What was your mission or goal?
- **ACTION**: Describe what you did. Explain the steps you took to tackle the challenge. Be specific and action oriented.
- **RESULT**: Explain what happened. What results did your actions achieve? How did things turn out?

You can use the STAR method to turn your experiences into powerful stories that showcase your skills and impress anyone you're talking to (and not just in interviews).

Here's an example:

SITUATION: At [HEI name], open days for prospective students were often hampered by staffing challenges. Inconsistent, last-minute rotas for various roles across faculties and departments led to confusion, duplicated efforts and, ultimately, a sub-par experience for visitors.
TASK: Recognising the need for improvement, I took the initiative to analyse the existing open-day staffing process. My goal was to create a more efficient, organised, and fair system for arranging cover across my faculty.
ACTION: I implemented the following steps:
 1 **Data Gathering and Analysis**: I surveyed colleagues about their availability and preferences for open days throughout the academic year.

I also analysed historical staffing data to identify patterns and areas for improvement.
2 **Collaboration and feedback**: I initiated a working group with representatives from across the faculty. Together, we brainstormed solutions, debated options, and ensured broad buy-in for the new system.
3 **Developing a framework**: Based on the data and feedback, I designed a flexible and transparent rota system. This included clear guidelines for assignment, consideration of individual preferences and workload, and a mechanism for volunteers to step forward.
4 **Implementation and communication**: I communicated the new system effectively to all faculty staff members, providing detailed instructions and training. I also implemented an online platform for easy access to the rota and facilitated open communication channels for feedback and adjustments.

RESULT: The new rota system was a resounding success. Open days ran smoothly with consistent staffing across my faculty. Faculty members appreciated the fairness and transparency of the system, and student feedback on the event experience improved significantly. This initiative was recognised by the institution's administration, highlighting my leadership skills, ability to drive process improvement, and talent for collaborative problem-solving. It is now being rolled out across other faculties and departments.

Always quantify your impact, if possible. Such as, 'an increase in volunteer enrolment', or 'improved student satisfaction metrics from open days'.

Keep your examples and your answers clear and concise. Focus on one specific example for each story and avoid jargon or technical terms.

'How would you...?'

How do you respond to a request from a senior manager to 'bend the rules'? How would you approach a colleague about an error they had made? How do you motivate others? These types of questions appear abstract, but the best answers you can give link the strategy or approach you would take to a similar real-life example. This demonstrates that you can do what you say you would do.

Your examples do not have to be directly related to your previous or current employment. David D. explains how you can draw on experience from your whole life:

> One of the best interview answers that I've ever had was in answer to someone being asked, 'What's your experience of managing budgets?' They said, 'Well, I'm the treasurer for my child's football team.' And no one forgot that candidate, no one forgot that answer to that question. It was a great answer. Earlier in my career, when I was asked, 'How do you motivate others?' Well, I was in my band, and I was writing the lyrics, and I was

singing, and I was booking the shows, and I was saying to my guys: 'We're going to go and play in Salisbury on a Monday night. There might only be five people there and we aren't going to get paid.' I think that probably taught me a lot more than I've even now realised and processed about leadership, when you don't have that hierarchy or authority behind you.

Emphasise, don't embellish

In an interview, focus on highlighting your contribution to projects, initiatives, or solutions. Often when talking about projects, candidates will focus on the team or department and talk in terms of what 'we' did. The panel needs to understand your contribution. What elements did **you** take responsibility for? What elements did **you** initiate? What was **your** approach? How did **you** engage with other members of the team? If you always talk in terms of 'we' and don't use I, the panel will not understand your strengths, skills, and potential.

Using 'we' can result in your contribution being under-represented. For example: 'We introduced a new way of processing applications from students for course transfers'. Here, the recruiter will have no idea what you did as part of this. The assumption would be that you were not very active in this project.

Notice the change here with the same example expressed differently:

> Based on feedback from students that I collated, I requested to my manager that we review the course transfer administration process. They and I, alongside the rest of the team, reviewed the process in relation to the feedback and we drafted a revised process that has now been implemented.

It's clear from this second version that you initiated this evidence-based process review and were a key contributor.

It is important, however, not to embellish your contributions. The panel will likely see through this. If they don't, you will be setting yourself up for failure in the role you have applied for as you won't be able to meet expectations. Either way, your professional reputation will be compromised, so don't do it.

If you are asked about your weaknesses, be honest but always explain how you are working to address them. When I am on a panel, I sense straight away that when people trot out stock answers, such as 'I am a perfectionist', they have lifted from a recruitment website. Only say 'I am a perfectionist' it is genuinely true, as your new manager will soon notice if your attention to detail doesn't match up.

The dreaded task

For my own interviews, I've had to do presentations, skills tests (in my case it was data analysis), and written tasks alongside face-to-face interviews. Hopefully, you will know in advance of the interview what, if any, tasks you will need to prepare for.

Once during an interview, whilst doing a data task, I had to look up how to generate a pivot table because I hadn't done one before. (I recommend against this. However, I can confirm that there is a handy wizard in Microsoft Excel that will take you through the process should you ever end up in that same pickle!)

A presentation is nearly always something you will be asked to prepare in advance. Here are some tips for presentations:

- Use an uncomplicated design.
- Choose a colour scheme that is not the colours of the organisation you are interviewing with, nor those of your current employer.
- Keep slides simple and visual.
- Don't read text from your slides – they should be illustrative prompts.
- Practice. Practice. Practice.
- Don't read straight from your notes – make eye contact with the panel for a more engaging delivery.
- When you are practicing, time yourself – the interview panel will cut you off if you run over. Part of the challenge is keeping to time.

Skills-based tasks are harder to prepare for. The job description and person specification can give you some helpful clues. If a job involves a lot of data analysis, you will need to be prepared to analyse and present some data.

Time management is important for skills-based tasks. Often, you are deliberately given insufficient time to complete all the tasks. This is so that the interviewers can see how you respond to time pressure and how you prioritise. For example, you are asked to reply to three emails and to summarise some data. In this scenario, I would recommend the data task is tackled before the emails. If you run out of time, it is better to have finished the data and written two emails than to have written three emails and not finished the data task.

Managing the nerves

One way to manage interview anxiety is to prepare well – both for the interview and for the logistics for getting there.

Interviews are nerve-wracking. Practicing with a mentor or colleague and thinking through potential examples you can use in advance can be helpful. Magda attributes self-belief to her success in securing her current role:

> I remember my interview really well, quite possibly because it was the most recent interview. I had quite a lot of practice with prior applications and interviews which helped me to learn my lines really well. I had the 'fake it 'til you make it' attitude. And I genuinely believed that I could do the job and that it would lead to other really cool things. The fact that I came from a different region in the UK, and a different country prior to that, was

proof that I was resilient, that I could handle stressful situations, that I liked change, and that I could manage and influence it whenever possible. I think they liked that. I've been in this role for just over two years.

Read the interview guidance carefully more than once. The guidance will tell you what to expect, where to go, and what to bring with you. For example, photo ID and some proof of your right to work in the UK (such as a passport) and your qualification certificates.

Look up the location online using a street view so you know what the building looks like. Work out where you're going to park or what train you'll catch and how to get from the carpark or the train station to the location. If you have all those arrangements clear in your head, then you can focus on the interview itself and manage some of the anxiety of going somewhere new.

You can look up the interview panel members on LinkedIn or the organisation's website, so you know who is interviewing and their areas of interest. If there are photos, that is even better as you will then know who you are looking out for.

Plan in advance what to wear. Don't underestimate the power of feeling confident and professional in your interview outfit. You are likely to get hot and flustered so don't wear a thick jumper or thermals.

On the day of the interview, try to get to the area early and find a café or place nearby you can wait. This will give you time to gather your thoughts after the stress of the journey. Building in a buffer of time also reduces the chances of you arriving late if there are traffic issues or train delays. Always show up at the interview venue five minutes before the appointed time. If you are going to be late, communicate immediately with the hiring manager/organisation to let them know.

When you know an interview panel member or the hiring manager

Some people find that knowing someone on the panel reassuring, but it could make your interview experience more challenging. You might feel extra pressure to perform well or be concerned about their pre-existing opinion of you. It can also lull you into a false sense of security and you might not give enough information about your experiences on the assumption that the panel already know you. A fair interview panel will assess you based on your application and your performance in the interview only, not anything they might know about you from another source. As a recruiter, I have had the experience of interviewing candidates I know. It is always disappointing when I am aware that a candidate has experience that would help them get the job, yet they don't bring it up during their interview because they know me.

I tell candidates that already know me, or members of the interview panel, that we will approach the interview as if we have never met before. I start the interview with formal introductions even if everyone in the room already knows each other. Not all interview chairs will do this. It is good practice to approach the interview as if the panel has no prior knowledge of you or your work. Avoid acronyms or if you do use them, explain them. Don't use names, instead refer to people as colleagues or by job title. Acting like you are being interviewed by people who know nothing about you gives you the best chance of securing the role.

Online interviews

If your interview is taking place online, arrange for a quiet place to do the interview. Ensure you have a decent internet connection and facility to use video. Dress as formally as you would for an in-person interview. There is something candidates often forget to do: tidy up the background! The best background is a plain wall. I've known of candidates who attended online interviews in their dressing gown, had inflammatory political slogans showing behind them, and had their personal pleasure toys in view on the bed behind them. Check your background!

Questions to ask the panel

It's great to have prepared questions in advance to ask the panel at the end of the interview. Be sure to tailor your questions to the specific role and team for which you are interviewing.

Good questions might include:

- What does a typical day look like for the person in this role?
- What are you looking for the successful candidate to achieve in the first three months with you?
- What are the team's priorities for the next six months?
- Why do you enjoy working here?

Questions not to ask include:

- What would the ideal candidate for this role look like? (I've been asked this and replied, 'That is laid out in the job description and person specification'. Avoid any questions about the role that has already been answered in the advert and interview pack.)
- What are the organisation's core values? (This is something that you should have looked up before coming to interview.)
- How do I compare with other candidates you've interviewed for this role? (An interview panel will never answer this so you should never ask it.)
- What is the starting salary for this role? (The pay grade will be specified in the job description. You can discuss whether entry can be at an increment point higher than the entry point of the grade with HR if you are offered the post.)

Afterwards

If you are successful, the chair of the interview panel is likely to call you directly to make a verbal offer. After the interview, keep your phone in hand as you won't want to miss that call! The verbal offer is not binding, and that phone call isn't the appropriate opportunity for asking detailed questions. You can request more time to think about the offer if you wish. Always give a deadline to the recruiting manager for when you will be back in touch with your decision (or they may give you one) and stick to it. When you verbally accept the role, you will be able to negotiate the finer details once you receive the written contract. Nothing is final until you have signed the contract so you are not beholden to the organisation if a reason comes up that you cannot proceed, for example, the organisation cannot accommodate your preferred working hours.

If you are unsuccessful, and particularly if you are an internal candidate, the chair of the panel may call you to explain that you were not successful on this occasion and to give you some feedback. Alternatively, and more commonly, especially if you are not already known to the recruiting manager, you will be notified by email that you have been unsuccessful. In both cases, I recommend contacting HR or the recruiting manager by email to request written feedback that you can reflect on once the initial disappointment has passed. Feedback will help you strengthen your future applications and interviews.

Whatever the outcome, be proud of yourself for the preparation and hard work you put into the application and interview. If you are not offered or do not accept the role, you have not failed or taken a step back. You have gained experience and built confidence just by applying for a new role. You should be proud of yourself for being bold and brave.

Digging deeper

How can you network with individuals working in the sector to gain insights and advice?

What specific actions can you take to address any identified skill gaps or weaknesses before your next interview?

What strategies will you adopt to manage interview anxiety and present yourself confidently?

Bookmark: jobs.ac.uk interview questions toolkit: https://career-advice.jobs.ac.uk/jobseeking-and-interview-tips/interview-questions-tool/. A toolkit to practise a wide range of common interview questions and suggested responses. It will help you prepare in advance and be equipped to answer a wide range of competency, motivation, and biographical questions.

Chapter 4

Strive, shine, soar
Getting noticed and making a visible impact

In the dynamic world of higher education, proactive self-development is key to getting noticed. This chapter is your roadmap to career advancement. It explores the importance of taking initiative, demonstrating leadership potential, and seeking mentorship to navigate the complexities of your organisation. Discover how to leverage transferable skills like problem-solving, communication and collaboration through taking initiative, getting involved in projects, and even leading teams. By continuously learning and adapting, you'll establish yourself as a valuable contributor and pave the way for a thriving career in higher education.

Be proactive

The only person who will prioritise your career is you. Be open to opportunities that might benefit you in your career. It isn't always immediately obvious where an opportunity might lead.

I was coordinating research degree admissions, enrolment, and administration when I was asked if I had capacity to support a new project with a new partner. I was approached as I have a background in taught course administration and because, at that time, the course administrators were tied up in exam boards. This project involved regular travel into London and working with the home admissions manager and a senior colleague in the student finance team to coordinate the verification and enrolment of a large volume of new students at short notice. We pooled our knowledge and resources during the summer and, by working together, we were successful in the task. It was a useful and rewarding experience for me. I enjoyed building new professional relationships, initiating a framework for working with the partner, supporting the project development, and expanding my knowledge of student funding and admissions.

Later that year, the deputy admissions manager post became vacant in the home admissions department at my institution. Before that project, I had only a few months of experience in research degree admissions. After it, I had a relationship with the admissions manager and a good understanding of a large number of non-standard qualifications and unusual immigration statuses. I had experience working with an important new partner and could demonstrate how I had contributed to the success of the project. This was crucial in my success in securing the deputy admissions manager role in the home admissions department.

David F.'s philosophy is to think strategically about opportunities:

> It's all of those little moments that give you the confidence to have those bigger moments, where you go, 'This is worth a punt, let's just go for it.' Things were pretty good in my previous role, and I wasn't actively looking for a new role, but an opportunity came, and I looked at it and thought, 'I should go for this, and I should leave while I'm still enjoying the current role.' I never want to get to the point where I resent the role I'm in.

And Simon reminds us we need to be our own champions:

> I think you have to be absolutely selfish in terms of taking every single ounce of opportunity that is offered.

It has been put to me that I only got the opportunity to work on the new partner project because I had experience of course administration and the head of registry knew of my skills. Absolutely. But that wasn't an accident. I sought out that role in course administration to build my technical and regulatory knowledge (even though it involved a pay reduction). I had worked hard in that role to build a reputation as an efficient, competent, and proactive course administrator who worked well in a team. So the opportunity to work on the project was not just based on circumstance. I had worked hard to put myself in a position to be considered. I also agreed to do it despite my existing work and the amount of travel it entailed.

Joanne has the same conviction:

> If there's something that you want to do or that you might be interested in, then volunteer. And sometimes it is a bit of extra work, but most of the time you'll get skills out of it, and you'll get recognised for it. I know it shouldn't necessarily be the case, but face recognition and talking to people is important because that's how people get to know who you are. And I think that's sometimes important.

Opportunities usually come from the groundwork you have laid in terms of your own professional development and relationships you have built. It's up to you whether you wish to take them and what you do with them, as Sarah explains:

> You might need to volunteer for a few things to get into opportunities where you raise your own profile and get to know other people who are in

similar management roles, even if they're not in similar work roles, because a lot of people management and leadership skills are transferable across lots of different disciplines.

Staying nestled in your comfort zone at work might feel safe, but progress and development demand a willingness to step outside your bubble. Mehmet explains how doing more of the same won't help in this area:

> You don't necessarily progress if you just do more at your current level. You might be in the administration space, but you won't necessarily get promoted or get a post at a higher grade if you just double the administration you're doing. That's about volume. The real lever is about the quality of your output, what you can do and how you go about doing it. For example, how can you elevate admin process or create a better workflow around it that makes it easier for others? If you want a promotion or if you want to progress, you have to work beyond your current level. It's not always true, but it's true most of the time that you have to work beyond your current level in order to show that you have the ability to do so. I used to hear, 'you don't need to do that' or 'that's not in your job description'. But that's how I expose myself to all types of the business. If I was happy to stay in my little box at the time, I would still probably be in that space and not have progressed.

By embracing new and potentially difficult tasks, you can access opportunities for growth. Challenging yourself with unfamiliar projects broadens your skillset, exposes you to diverse perspectives, and fosters resilience in the face of obstacles. Stepping outside your comfort zone is about taking calculated risks and a having growth mindset that understands that the true potential for advancement lies beyond the boundaries of the familiar. So, take a deep breath, embrace the temporary discomfort, and take action.

Secondments

One advantage of working in higher education is that it offers potential opportunities for secondment posts. In the case of a secondment, staff are able to apply and interview for a temporary role and, should they take up the position, their original role is protected. The employer is required to keep their original post or replace it with something commensurate after the secondment ends.

For Joanne, secondments have been the key to progression, development, and a fulfilling career:

> I can't emphasise enough how much secondments have helped me in terms of professionalism and professional practice. I've had three successive

secondments now and the last six years has been transformative for me in terms of learning new skills, developing myself and understanding how to manage different people – going from central to research to school roles and getting that depth and those transferable skills and the understanding of how different places work. And what I've got out of it is that the ability to know that my career is in HE and I always knew it was, but I want to stay, and this is what I want to do. And I feel confident now that I could go into most other areas and be able to go into that place and pick things up, not necessarily the skills to do the job but be able to manage those processes. Getting the opportunity to set up a brand-new research centre from scratch was so good for the way I see myself at work and how I've developed. And it's given me much more confidence.

For David F. a secondment was an opportunity to gain line management experience:

I knew that I wanted to manage. For me, it was about leading a team and growing and learning with that team and having people to bounce ideas off. I remember vividly, every single job description that I looked at and applied for stated: 'management experience required'. And I was like, how do I get management experience to be a manager? This is a real blocker and I'm sure lots of people come up against this. So I started looking at different opportunities such as management qualifications. Then, out of the blue, I saw a maternity cover role and secondment within the university which sounded ideal because it was just a year: a try before you buy thing. If they hate me or it doesn't work out, I thought, I can go back. But also, this job would give me a year of experience so I could use it as a test if I think I'm good at it and I'm able to achieve and move forward. So it was just one of those things where stars align and you're like, this is the right thing and there's nothing to lose from that kind of role. So I had a very open conversation with the recruiting manager and with my manager and said, 'This is what I want to do.' I was very upfront about it all. When I interviewed, I was mindful that I didn't have the exact experience both within the job and within the management role, but I just tried to show what I would do and where I would add value.

David D. was looking to broaden his experience:

A secondment opportunity came up in our registry team, in what was then the academic policy and standards team. This was student complaints, academic appeals, dealing with the OIA [Office of the Independent Adjudicator] and a few bits of policy stuff. And I thought, well, I did complaints before, I quite enjoyed that, I'll have a pop at this. It was a maternity cover secondment. I was delighted to get it. It was initially for eight or nine months. But pretty quickly, a couple of members of the team left and I was able to secure a permanent role in the team at the grade above.

Engage with others in your field

By interacting with others across the sector, you will encounter different approaches, experiences, and viewpoints. This sparks creativity and challenges assumptions, leading to innovative solutions you might not otherwise have come up with. Engaging with your sector gives you insight into emerging developments, best practices, and how to leverage connections. Sharing knowledge benefits everyone. Sharing your expertise, participating in discussions, and offering support to others benefits the entire community, fostering a culture of continuous improvement and innovation. Engaging with others builds relationships, strengthens your professional network, and enhances your visibility. This translates into recognition, potential collaboration opportunities and, ultimately, career advancement.

Getting noticed is just the beginning. David F. reminds us that relationships are vital:

> There has to be something in it for both parties. It couldn't just be a case of, 'I want to do this project and it's only going to benefit me.' There has to be a trade-off. I think they're really important things that go unnoticed, those relationships, and forging them and building that rapport.

LinkedIn is a great space in which to do this informally and across professional divisions. A number of sector organisations have forums, committees, networks and working groups that are opportunities for engagement. Some are sector-wide, for example, UKCISA (UK Council for International Student Affairs), AHEP (Association of Higher Education Professionals), Advance HE, and AMOSSHE (Association of Managers of Student Services in Higher Education). Others are more specialists, such as UCAS (Universities and Colleges Admissions Service), HELOA (Higher Education Liaison Officers Association – the professional association of staff in higher education who work in student recruitment, outreach, marketing, and admissions), NASMA (National Association of Student Money Advisors), HESPA (Higher Education Strategic Planners Association), and SCONUL (Society of College, National and University Libraries). *(Higher education adores an acronym!).*

Self-directed learning

There are lots of opportunities for self-directed learning and development. Dive into bite-sized skills-based courses, from IT to marketing, available on the web. Find out what training opportunities are available to you through your organisation's HR/organisational development team. Explore free or low-cost courses from top universities and institutions on platforms like OpenLearn and FutureLearn. Read books, blogs, and articles to enhance your knowledge. Gain insights from industry leaders through webinars, recorded talks (such as TEDx), and live sessions offered by professional organisations.

You can learn at your own pace, schedule, and preferred format. Many options are free or affordable, making upskilling accessible. Identify areas you want to improve or build your knowledge in and choose resources accordingly. Actively engage with the content, participate in discussions, and apply what you learn.

Mehmet shares some of the resources he finds helpful:

> Looking at things outside of the higher education sphere is always helpful. I listen to a lot of lifestyle and self-development podcasts. Trying to understand how others have gone about their own journey is quite helpful. It's not always the same context, but there is a lot of transferrable advice and these methods of problem-solving or the frameworks to break things down, codify them, are helpful. I suppose being interested in that kind of continuous improvement has been my way forward in this. Conferences and things like that, exposing yourself to different ideas and exposing yourself to different personalities is helpful. I link into the sector thought leadership such as any Wonkhe articles, any kind of public commentary around that. HEPI [Higher Education Policy Institute] blogs are really important for colleagues within more strategic roles. Subscribe to those kinds of newsletters and you'll learn a lot more about life outside of your own institution. That's how I stay in touch with the rest of the sector.

Take initiative to solve problems and improve processes

Creative problem-solving, within the framework of rules and regulations, is an everyday challenge in higher education, but not everyone is good at it. It's an opportunity for innovation and impact, as Sarah explains:

> So many times, we are navigating challenges that we don't know the answer to, the industry doesn't know the answer to, and certainly individual universities, individual departments individual projects don't either. You do need to be aware of what's going on and to be solutions-focused because you do need to find answers that aren't necessarily there.

You often have to be creative in coming up with ways to achieve an outcome. But you also have to work with what is immovable (such as, regulations) and the processes you may have to follow to get to the outcome. To succeed in professional services, you have to see the rules and regulations as something to be grappled, negotiated, and worked with, rather than a barrier or something that's stopping you from finding a solution. Magda shares her preferred analogy:

> It's trying to skilfully manoeuvre around the obstacles. Higher education administration is like gymnastics.

When reviewing existing processes, focus on offering constructive challenges. People are protective of their knowledge and the processes they use. Jenny's strategy is to ask questions:

> I drive people mad. I ask so many questions. You can come at it from a position of naivety, 'Oh, sorry. It's new to me. There's probably a really good reason that I don't understand, but can you explain why it's being done like that?' More often than not, it's because that's how it's always been done so people just carry on without challenging it. Nothing frustrates me more. Find out if there's a better way. Of course don't just tell someone you think their process is rubbish – ask why they're doing it like that. That's how things are improved and processes are made better.

Stepping back

Stepping back to assess both successes and areas for growth can lead to exciting developments and skill-building opportunities. Jeanette explains how she and her team do this to facilitate continuous improvement:

> We do a lot of reflection, whether that's post clearing or it's after an event or in monthly meetings. This is because we carry out a lot of development of new systems and we are becoming more and more lean. There's a lot of pressure out there. I see it as an opportunity to get people involved in exciting stuff, not just in their processing, but it's about what we can do better. Yes, it's great to talk about what went right and what was good, and we need to focus on that because that boosts us. But actually, it's really important to do a review of what can we do better and, with that, get people to chip in, volunteer to build their skills and abilities. We should never stop learning or trying new things. It's a bit of a rolling, ongoing thing that we have built in, and people know it's coming, so they keep thinking like that. They're constantly reviewing, tweaking, adapting, improving, and then telling us about it, and we go, 'Oh, that's amazing.' And then they get lifted, and then they want to make another change. So, there you go. It's like a constant improvement process.

Simon suggests greater focus would be beneficial:

> I think we need to be better in terms of really looking for where consistency is important and where we can streamline things and where we can learn

from best practice. It's something we trot out a lot, but we don't often take enough time to stop and pause and look at where things are going really well and where they're not going well and what should we be learning from those.

Magda reminds us that our values and belief in our work can be hugely motivating when we take a moment to reflect:

> I very often find myself so bogged down in the detail that I forget why I'm really there, what it is that we're trying to do and all the good that comes out of it. This is wrong because it strips the job of its core purpose and meaning, and what we do should have a lot of meaning.

Bring solutions to the table

Be someone who brings solutions rather than problems to the table. 'Nobody told me', 'the faculty/department/other team/organisation should have done this', and phrases like this shift responsibility away from you, suggesting you need explicit instructions for every action. This portrays a passive and uninvested attitude and hinders your development. An example of this, which can be particularly annoying, is when colleagues say that the student records system did something wrong or won't do what they want it to do. My response to that is to tell them that the student records system is not a sentient being! It can only do what we ask it to with the information we enter. Peter shares this frustration:

> A pet hate is when academics talk about the university as, 'The university won't let me.' I always say, 'You're the university!' If you break down that barrier and say that you're part of the university, we're all the university, it does help. People will always moan about something, but I don't believe the whole idea of blaming others is healthy, especially when those people are not necessarily to blame.

Taking ownership doesn't mean doing everything yourself. It's about being responsible, proactive, and contributing to the team's success, even if tasks fall outside your specific job description. Colleagues and managers respect those who take responsibility and see projects through.

When you take ownership for your actions and decisions, you demonstrate reliability and accountability. This builds trust and enhances your credibility and reputation. Sarah cautions:

> Don't just bring me problems. I'm perfectly happy with a challenge, but at least have a think about what you think might be a good way of doing it. It doesn't matter if it wasn't right, but you've gone through some of the thought process and you've given it a bit of thought, which is all I want.

If you are solutions-focused, you do not dwell on a problem and complain to your colleagues and managers. Rather, you view challenges as opportunities. It's a skill that can be developed with practice. The more you focus on solutions, the easier it will become. Brainstorming strategies, evaluating options, and making informed recommendations are the keystones to a solutions-focused approach.

Learning from experienced professionals

Mentoring and coaching offer a wealth of knowledge and support that can help you accelerate your professional growth by learning from experienced professionals. The Chartered Institute of Personnel and Development (CIPD) (the professional body for HR and people development) defines mentoring and coaching as 'development approaches based on the use of one-to-one conversations to enhance an individual's skills, knowledge or work performance' (CIPD, 2023).

I've had some amazing mentors in my career, and their guidance has been invaluable. In sectors like the public sector, where formal training resources may be limited, mentorship becomes even more crucial. By learning from experienced professionals, you can gain insights, avoid pitfalls, and develop effective strategies for success. Embrace the power of mentoring and embark on a journey of continuous learning and growth. I agree with Sarah that there are a lot of people who are willing to mentor and guide others:

> We should be encouraging people to seek out mentors, coaches, and actually push it because nobody will offer it. There are lots of people who would be prepared to help you and develop that if only you knew that was possible. Tell people, it is possible. There are lots of people who would be happy to help you.

Finding a good mentor for you

A mentor is someone you look up to and admire, someone who's more experienced and has a career trajectory you aspire to follow. Identifying potential mentors can be done through informal networking, observing professionals in your field and browsing profiles on platforms like LinkedIn. Seek individuals who share your interests and passions and think about preparing a structured proposal outlining your strategy, expectations, the areas you want to focus on, and the frequency of meetings.

Approaching a mentor with confidence

It can be intimidating approaching someone to ask them to mentor you. Most people are open to sharing their knowledge and experience, and many are flattered to be asked to mentor, but remember to be respectful of their time and demonstrate your commitment to making the mentor relationship productive and mutually beneficial. I advise you to approach the conversation with a specific proposal and clear expectations. In your proposal, present your goals, the support you seek, and the structure you envision for the mentorship. This demonstrates your maturity and professionalism, making the potential mentor more receptive to your request. Once the relationship has begun, continue to be mindful of their time and avoid bombarding them with emails or expecting them to solve every problem you face. Focus on specific areas where their guidance will be most valuable.

When meeting with your mentor, come equipped with a clear agenda and specific questions. Discuss the topics you identified in your proposal, actively listen to their insights, and take notes to retain valuable information. Be open to their feedback and suggestions. Demonstrate your willingness to apply their advice in your professional endeavours. Show gratitude for their time and commitment to your growth and maintain open communication to ensure the mentorship continues to deliver benefits for both parties.

Learning from the anti-mentors

There are the managers and senior colleagues from whom we learn much of what not to do and I call these managers our 'anti-mentors'. I agree with Magda that, as unpleasant as the experience can be, we can always learn something from such anti-mentors:

> Bad managers are important. This is my conclusion. Bad managers are probably more important than good managers as they force change in us, and they show us what we should not be as human beings, managers and leaders.

Jenny learnt what not to do from one of her anti-mentors:

> The worst manager I have ever had used to walk through the office and say, 'I know you all hate me – that means I'm doing a good job.' We were literally managed through fear, and I learned that this is the absolute worst way to manage anyone. And then a lovely new manager came, and everyone learned that if you treat people well, they work hard. We all wanted to do a really good job for that person and would have worked all hours to get things done, because they were really understanding and respectful.

Even if your current manager isn't the epitome of positive leadership, you can still learn from their experiences and mistakes. Observe their strengths and weaknesses and identify areas where you can improve your own leadership style.

Demonstrating leadership skills

It is almost impossible to progress in seniority in higher education without supervising or coordinating other people. To succeed in all forms of leading others, you need to develop and enhance your leadership skills. Even academics have to do this. Course leaders don't lead courses. They lead a group of people through a complex web of delivery, monitoring, teaching, learning, and administration without having line management responsibility for, or authority over, any of them. Mehmet is well versed in navigating this minefield:

> At universities, after a certain level, you do have to usually take on teams in order to progress. But it was a case of proving myself first as a planning manager and then owning lots of processes and initiatives. Being accountable for them. I wasn't necessarily line managing lots of people at this point, but I was overseeing the work of lots of individuals outside of my direct responsibility in a matrix kind of way, owning and leading different initiatives and processes.
>
> It's a case of demonstrating through your work, through your output, that you can manage people, you can manage big initiatives, you can manage projects and you can influence other people without necessarily just being their line manager. That's probably a really important skill to note for anyone, that ability to work outside of your team, because you have to have that wide view of the world. It's not just about what you or your direct team does.

Every manager starts their career not being a manager. We all start our careers without any responsibility for other humans and at some point, we stepped into a supervisory role. Sometimes it's accidental: you end up promoted into a post, acting up into a post, or there's a restructure that deposits you into a management post when you weren't quite expecting it. Alternatively, and for most people, it's a conscious decision to transition into a management role.

Managing people is not something that comes from being really good at your job. Just because you are a high-performing systems developer does not mean you are going to be highly proficient at coordinating a team of systems developers. Managing people requires its own unique combination of skills. Where there is little in the way of budget or scope for management and leadership training (especially *before* you take up a management role), as is generally the case across the public sector, as professionals in higher education we must rely on our wits to navigate this new world. As the Chartered Management Institute (CMI) has shown us in their recent research, 82 per cent of managers have no idea what they're doing when they become a manager (CMI, 2023). In other words, they are winging it. I was definitely in that category.

Jenny asks:

> How do people know what to do? And how do people know how to do it well? I wouldn't want to just do an adequate job. I want to get the best out of people and really help them to be good and get on and better.

The short answer is that often we don't. David D. remembers the advice he received from others when he took on his first-line management role:

> Initially, I was quite a reluctant line manager. I was in a position where there were five of us in our team and in the new structure, there would still be five of us, so if one of us didn't apply to be the team leader, one of us would be at risk of redundancy or redeployment. Two of us applied and I got it, but I didn't feel comfortable applying for it and I didn't ever feel aspirations in that direction, so the first thing I asked was, 'What training do I get?' I was told, 'So you might want to establish a spreadsheet or something, just to track when your team asks for leave. And if anyone's off sick too often, you might want to have a bit of a word.'

People management isn't a skill you can instantly acquire and become an expert at through a qualification. It's a skillset that you can develop even if you haven't held a formal management position before. If you're considering transitioning into management and you're worried about convincing a hiring manager that you're the right person to lead their team, remember that management is all about communicating, collaborating, problem-solving, projecting confidence, and empowering your team members. These are skills that you can develop and showcase through various avenues. It could be through projects you've coordinated, supervising volunteers or temporary staff or leading initiatives for change. All these actions demonstrate the traits and skills that managers need, and they don't necessarily have to stem from direct supervisory experience. It's all about your mindset and how you present yourself. Focus on developing the transferable skills that will prove you have the potential to be an exceptional leader.

David F. highlights ways to get some experience and exposure:

> There are opportunities that everybody gets when your line manager is off, or your manager might ask you to present on something. And I remember my manager being off for a while and I stepped in and was asked to act up at that point. And that gives you that confidence to handle these meetings or deliver such and such in that way. So there are small things that build over time as well and give you opportunities to capture some experience of that level without actually being that person. For me, there were loads of those opportunities where I might go into a meeting and think, 'There's going to be loads of more senior people here, and I've got to talk about this.' And I would come out and think, 'I did all right.'

Even if you don't take up a line management position, remember that a broad portfolio of skills is needed to navigate any complex organisation. Developing your leadership and management skills will help you to successfully navigate internal politics, collaborative projects and partnership working. This applies across the academic-professional services continuum.

Digging deeper

What solutions could you propose to difficulties in your current role that would demonstrate your critical thinking and leadership skills?

In what ways are you taking initiative to join or lead projects that align with your interests and demonstrate your skills? How are you contributing effectively and collaboratively?

Who are individuals within your institution whose experience and values align with yours? How can you initiate a conversation with them?

Read: The Higher Education Policy Institute (HEPI) was established in 2002 to shape the higher education policy debate through evidence and has a blog. Available at: www.hepi.ac.uk.

Have a go: 21 Coach Yourself Questions from Amazing If. Available at: www.amazingif.com/wp-content/uploads/2022/07/AI_21CoachYourself Questions_RGB_2022-07-08.pdf.

References

CIPD, 2023. Factsheet: coaching and mentoring. *CIPD*, 2 August. Available at: <www.cipd.org/uk/knowledge/factsheets/coaching-mentoring-factsheet/>.

CMI, 2023. New study: bad managers and toxic work culture causing one in three staff to walk. *CMI*, 16 October. Available at: <www.managers.org.uk/about-cmi/media-centre/press-releases/bad-managers-and-toxic-work-culture-causing-one-in-three-staff-to-walk/>.

Chapter 5

Empower, engage, elevate
Managing people and teams

This chapter provides a comprehensive guide to navigating the exciting – and sometimes challenging – world of managing a team. It delves into the importance of listening to team members, actively learning from them, and building a foundation of trust. We will consider why taking time to understand the team and fostering clear communication are crucial before implementing changes. Setting realistic expectations sets both you and your team up for success.

This chapter champions delegation, empowerment, and inclusivity as core principles. It will show you how to be a supportive leader who celebrates achievements and trusts your team's abilities. By creating a culture of open dialogue, shared responsibility, and continuous learning, you'll be able to build a successful and thriving team. Remember, leading a team is a means to achieving strategic goals. By effectively guiding your team, you'll gain the freedom to lead in the way that best suits your strengths and your team's dynamics.

Beginning

At the start of your new role leading a team, you will no doubt be super keen to dive in, make a positive impact, and address areas for development. What is the first thing you should do when you start a new job as a manager? This answer might surprise you.

Nothing…

…except listen and learn. As David F. warns:

> Typically speaking, you're inheriting an existing team with existing processes. All of those things come with different challenges. For me, the hardest initial things to get over are cultural aspects within the setup and the mentality of the team, and the sharing of knowledge, because people are quite protective of knowledge.

Listen and learn. Keep your counsel. Bite your tongue. Keep detailed notes on all the things that are jumping out at you. Keep listening. Listen a bit more. Even when you think you can see what needs to be done, wait! Listen and learn some more. No one appreciates a new manager who comes in and immediately starts changing things as Magda explains:

> Sometimes people are too eager to prove themselves whereas they should actually hold back a little. I know that it can be hard. When you come into a new role everything is fresh and you feel instinctively where improvements should, in your mind, be made. But I would focus on understanding the process first. And taking as many notes as possible so those thoughts or ideas don't get forgotten as the weeks go by. Once I'm confident that I understand the process, I'd revisit my notes, have a chat with my manager and suggest some changes. Or maybe keep a list of some really cool ideas and share them gradually, to keep the momentum going.

Jeanette outlines the unlearning we need to do when we start working with a team:

> You bring your own skills and abilities to the table, but you are also bringing your subconscious behaviour from your previous experiences. And that's exactly what it is. It's the unlearning of 'this is what we did over here' or 'that's the team I'm used to'. And it's a bit like, 'Okay, what's the situation here?' What are the concerns? What are the people like? What is the common goal? And then it's about creating this new team because it is a team. It's really important, I think, if you're a leader or manager, to be a part of the team, and for everyone to know their responsibilities and their ownership. And then when it comes to difficult decisions, it's important to be the person stepping up to make those decisions.

Getting to know your team members

Making an active effort to get to know each member of your team is key. When I join a new team, I meet each person face to face (online or in person) for an individual conversation. I give them a quick summary of my background and philosophy then ask them five questions that frame our discussion:

1 How did you get here, in this role, in this organisation, in higher education more generally? (Here I'm inviting them to share their career journey to date.)
2 What are your aspirations for progression and development and how can I, as your manager, support your professional development goals?
3 What do we currently do best as a team?
4 What do we need to do better as a team?
5 What can I do to help you be more effective in your role?

For example, when I did this with one particular team, they all highlighted a range of complementary themes around what they were doing really well, which helped me understand what they took pride in and what they were focusing their attention on. Additionally, every single member of this team (around 30 people) shared the same suggestion of what they felt we needed to do better. It told me exactly where I need to start.

Management manners

Employees thrive under supportive leadership that prioritises clear communication and values their input. This means having managers who are transparent, honest, and open. We expect fairness, consistency, and a sense of being valued from our leaders. Additionally, empathy and emotional intelligence are crucial for fostering a positive work environment. David Dunbar (2014) calls these behaviours, 'management manners'. I find this concept helpful for articulating the elements that combine to represent positive and impactful management. Let's consider each facet in more detail.

Communication

As David F. explains, communication is central to good management:

> The dysfunctional teams are the ones with managers who don't properly communicate and set out clear expectations. So if the team doesn't know what's being asked of them or it's not communicated in the right way, it could be a real problem.

Aim for transparency and frank communication in all aspects of business (goals, decisions, challenges, and priorities). Encourage team member input to discussion and genuinely consider their perspectives in decision-making and implementation. Foster a culture of open feedback (both ways) offering constructive criticism and welcoming suggestions and critique. There will be things you have to keep to yourself, and transparency does not mean disclosing confidential information.

Effective communication includes consistency and decisiveness. My most stressful experiences of being managed centred on managers who were inconsistent or indecisive. One day it would be fine for me to do something, another it wouldn't, with no logic behind either. Together, indecision and inconsistency are a toxic combination that leaves team members with no idea of what they need to do and vulnerable to excessive criticism.

Being decisive can be difficult, but it is good practice always to make a decision instead of stalling indefinitely. How much information do we need to choose? You need to make a judgment based on the information available, policy, process, business need, and circumstances. You need enough information to make a decision, but if you stall in the hope of securing 100 per cent of the information you need, you will miss the opportunity or create bigger future challenges for everyone. Every decision involves some risk – as a manager you need to own that risk. If you change your mind, or circumstances dictate that your choice must change, always take responsibility for that. Too often I've had a manager tell me to do something then later deny that they gave the instruction. (If you have a manager who does this regularly, email them after the verbal instruction just to confirm that they have asked you to do x.)

Listen

Listening is a huge element of good communication. Being a good listener isn't just about being quiet while someone talks. It's about actively engaging with their message, understanding their meaning, and facilitating a meaningful conversation. It's an intentional process. It's listening to learn rather than to respond. And it is hard. It is something I am always working on being better at.

To actively listen, avoid distractions, maintain eye contact, and actively engage with the speaker's words and emotions. Avoid interrupting, offer empathy, and use non-verbal cues like nodding and open body language to signal your attentiveness. Demonstrate understanding by reflecting, paraphrasing, and asking clarifying questions. Approach the conversation with an open mind, avoiding judgment and allowing the speaker space and time to express themselves.

Simon has embedded this approach in this practice:

> I've always talked with my teams about recognising people's styles, recognising how long people might need to process something, and not just following the loudest voice in the room.

The benefits of active listening extend far beyond improved communication. It boosts your productivity by ensuring you gather accurate information and avoid misunderstandings. It enhances your ability to influence, persuade, and negotiate by building trust and fostering collaboration. Additionally, it helps you navigate conflict effectively, leading to stronger relationships and a more positive overall working relationship.

David F. aligns listening with understanding:

> I think understanding what people's motivations are comes into it. So, why are you in the job? Does it work for you now? Can you disappear off and get home quick if that's what you need? Or, no, this is a stepping stone for me to the next thing. So it's understanding that dynamic and how you can tune that up or down depending on the individual or balance the team accordingly. And on a personal level, too, I think it's really important to understand. It's the small things that go a long way, like remembering that somebody does a certain thing a certain way or their kids names.

Set clear expectations

Be clear with what you are expecting from your team, not just in terms of expected outcomes, but vision, direction, and underlying principles. Give them sufficient context to effectively meet your expectations.

Mehmet has a methodical approach:

> Probably the biggest thing that I do is try to break things down. I work backwards from the output that we need, break it down bit by bit and codify everything: this is one part of the process and that is the other part of the process. I will ask: is it this area that needs the work or is it that area that needs the work? Also, how do we support it? What can we do? So it involves a lot of thinking and breaking down of things and contemplation. But it's around that, that we can increase the team's understanding, because that's all that it comes down to. Ultimately, the ideas might be in your head, you might already know what the end looks like, but the others are going to have to bring that forward and you need to collaborate and be aligned through the process to get there.

I start every training session, policy discussion, and process change or review with the 'why' before I dive into the 'how'. People thrive on purpose and understanding the 'why' behind tasks significantly impacts the emotional response. When people understand the significance of their work, they are more likely to engage wholeheartedly, accept guidance, and strive to meet the targets and deadlines set, even if they don't agree with these.

Jeanette encourages her team to be innovative, vocal, and creative within the framework she outlines:

> By allowing people to suggest, propose, be involved, grow and be easy-going in your leadership, in other words, not sweating the small stuff and not just directing them like a director, you are creating the allowance to say no. I have no problem being really straight down the line and just saying 'no, we can't do this', or 'no, that's not a good idea' or whatever, but I always back it up with the reason why and I'll be authentic. But it is also because I am easy going and I care and I drive them. Because I do all of that, no one takes the 'no' badly as they get so much. So I'm not a 'no' person, I'm a 'yes, hey, let's try and do it' person. But when it's a no, it's a no. I guess you have nowhere to go if you're being really negative. No one's going to come to you for anything if you're just constantly scary and saying no to everything.

Whatever your institution's approach to induction, probation, and annual appraisals, try not to fall into the trap of thinking of them as 'tick box exercises'. They are an opportunity to frame your expectations through co-creation of clear targets, support the development of your team members, and monitor their progress against objectives. Optimise your use of these tools.

Structure dialogue

Preparation is key. At the beginning of each week, I use these three questions to frame my team meetings:

- What was the highlight of last week?
- What's your focus and potential biggest challenge this week?
- How can I support you to achieve your priorities this week?

I like these questions because they enable me to structure the conversation and make sure that we have a constructive discussion in the time that we have together. It gives the team an opportunity for active reflection on the previous week and takes a momentary pause to recognise the positive things that they have achieved. We're all guilty of skimming over successes and reflections. Taking that time to reflect gives a chance to focus on and celebrate some of those small wins. In thinking about the coming week, I'm asking the team to consider current projects and not just think about what they need to do as the next task. It encourages them to own their workload management and to engage with me around what support they might need rather than expecting me to know when they're overstretched or when they could do with another colleague supporting them on something.

I also have fortnightly one-to-one sessions with the team members who report to me directly. It is important to build this time into your schedule however busy you are. Some rescheduling is inevitable but only cancel when absolutely unavoidable. It's important to be consistent and make space for conversations about individual challenges, team priorities, and development plans. This is even more important when working with a hybrid or cross-campus model whereby you might not see your team members very often and/or the team might not be together very often. I manage a team across two campuses that are quite far apart, and this is something we are very conscious of.

Joanne values individual conversations with her team members:

> I'm a big fan of having those one-to-one conversations. I think the PDR [Performance and Development Review] process is important, but I don't think having conversations two or three times a year is enough. I want to know what you're doing; I want to know how you're doing it, what help you need. Let's have a look at what the next 12 months is going to look like. What do we need to get there? What do you need from me in order to do that? Those conversations should be happening all the time. And I think it's good for staff to be recognised. And I think often academics will refer to them as backroom staff or admin. But actually, I think professional services need to be recognised for what they do. I'm a big believer in pushing out what the team have done.

If this sort of regular contact is maintained, there won't be any surprises on either side when you carry out formal appraisals/review meetings.

Inclusivity and fairness

We all value a manager who is fair and inclusive in their approach. Not everyone processes information in the same way. Magda's experience highlights the importance of an inclusive approach to management:

> I don't like it when someone just stands over me and explains a system or a process and just talks at me. I will focus more on how they say stuff than what it is that they say. I'd rather they either gave me the guidance or allowed me to write things down properly or send me a memo. It's just the way I'm wired.

Magda's story reminds us that there are many learning preferences and approaches. One action that I took away from our conversation was the importance of embedded the principles of Universal Design for Learning (UDL) into training that I deliver (CAST, 2024). This means providing multiple ways for people to learn and participate, so everyone has an equal chance to succeed. True inclusion is about actively fostering an environment where everyone feels valued, respected, and empowered to contribute their unique talents and perspectives.

By welcoming and celebrating the diverse backgrounds, experiences, and identities within our teams, we unlock a wealth of fresh ideas and perspectives. This diversity of thought not only enhances creativity and problem-solving, but also strengthens our ability to understand and meet the needs of a multicultural society.

Understanding our own positioning is an important aspect, as David D. explains:

> I am always conscious that I am a cishet, middle-class British white guy and I always worry about imposing myself in a space or making assumptions. And it's an interesting tension, because the labour around inclusivity, and particularly EDI [equality, diversity and inclusion], should not solely fall upon marginalised groups, but equally, I never want to impose myself or make assumptions or appropriate. I'm reflecting on that on a regular basis. ['Cishet' describes someone who is cisgender (their gender identity corresponds to their sex assigned at birth) and heterosexual.]

Genuine inclusion requires going beyond superficial gestures. We must be mindful of both our conscious and unconscious biases (affinity, confirmation, and proximity), dismantling any systemic barriers that may disadvantage certain groups. This includes recognising and accommodating the individual needs of our team members, whether it be navigating language barriers, managing caring responsibilities or adapting to flexible work arrangements where possible. Simon learnt this the hard way:

> I think the juggle is really important. You have to be really careful in terms of recognising where your entire workforce is at. If you assume that that person will pick this task up because they haven't got these needs, does that

then create resentment in the team? And if you've got people who have got childcare responsibilities and they're functioning in a particular way, is that to the detriment of someone else? It's really about having those conversations. The worst thing that you can do, which I did in one of my early roles, was say, 'Just work it out amongst yourselves.' Then you've got people knocking on your door going, 'I can't go on holiday because this person's booked the same time, and they say they have to have that time because of their children.' It created this absolute beast of a situation just because I was too cowardly to deal with it.

Inclusivity for one member of staff could be detrimental to another. Balance and diplomacy are required. Colleagues on part-time contracts can find it especially hard to feel part of a team, to access information, take up development opportunities and progress in seniority. Whilst approaches to flexible working have rapidly evolved across the higher education sector since the COVID-19 pandemic, traditional organisational structures that anticipate professional staff working across 'core' hours (often Monday to Friday, 8am/9am to 4pm/5pm) remain. The language we use – full time and part time – still implies a degree of commitment, this is despite research showing that reduced working hours usually equate to greater productivity. Teams or organisations can inadvertently marginalise part-time or flexible workers because they're not always working across those 'core' hours and so can be perceived as not working as hard (Lawrence & Corwin, 2023).

David D.'s conversation with colleagues highlighted some of the challenges:

I was talking to two part-time colleagues recently about career moves. Because I've been here for a while, people often come to me and ask me questions such as: 'Where should I not apply to?' 'What should I do?' or 'Is this a good job?' And I find it so difficult with part-time colleagues because they'll tell me that all the jobs are full-time and all you can do is say, 'Well, you might find someone who can do a job share.' I've floated the idea with our HR to establish a database or a repository of job-share opportunities so if you are in this situation and you can find a buddy who's at the same grade, wants the same kind of thing, it's going to make your chances much better of getting a role and it's going to make you more comfortable. It's so ridiculous and inflexible that most management roles are full time. So much of the way we do stuff in universities, particularly Russell group universities, is not necessary anymore. And I get that no one's has the headspace to rethink it, but maybe sometimes it's an excuse, isn't it?

On her return from maternity leave, Jenny reduced her working hours and found it extremely challenging:

I very quickly realised that you couldn't just stay late to finish something off because you've got to go back and pick your baby up. You can't get there early because you've got a baby at home. I had been the go-to person. People would say, 'Jenny will know that. Jenny will get that done.' Well, I couldn't do that anymore because I wasn't there half the week. And then when I was there, I had to leave dead on time because I had to pick my child up. So I thought, I can't carry on here. I can't bear it. I can't bear to be the person that doesn't know everything anymore! I saw a part-time job advertised at another university so I applied for it, but I didn't really think I would get it. I went for the interview, and they offered me the job straight away. I asked for the weekend to think about it as I was leaving somewhere where I was so comfortable. It was a big decision to leave. I've realised since I left that the issue wasn't that I wasn't the go-to person there anymore, the issue was working part time! I think I will always find working part time a challenge because you just feel like you're just putting in half the effort whatever you're doing, wherever you are. I'm not fully doing my job at home, being a mum, because I'm only there half the time and I'm not fully doing what I'm doing at work because I can never quite finish something because I've got to pick up the kids. But I think that's probably quite a common feeling with working part time – or just being a working mum – and I'm used to it now. It's definitely got better, since the pandemic and working from home, because there is more of a balance. But I would say working part time is really hard.

Ultimately, fostering a truly inclusive workplace isn't just about doing the right thing; it's about unlocking the full potential of our collective talent. When everyone feels seen, heard and valued, everyone thrives, and our organisations reap the rewards of a truly diverse and dynamic workforce. Achieving that will also make your job easier as everyone will feel more comfortable in their role.

Discussion of underrepresented groups and those with protected characteristics tends to focus on categorisations of individual characteristics. 'Assemblages of disadvantage' is a way to think of how the different disadvantages a person might face might interact and multiply their vulnerability to discrimination (Harwood et al., 2017). For example, a physically disabled woman might be seen as dependent, making it harder to be seen as a leader, even if her abilities are excellent. Gender bias, stereotyping around disability, and accessibility challenges compound to form a greater disadvantage than each element alone. In another scenario, a prayer room that is only accessible by stairs creates a barrier for someone who uses a mobility aid. This essentially excludes them from a space designated for their religious practice.

David D. takes a broad view in his approach to inclusive practice:

Inclusivity is really important to me, whether that is about protected characteristics or whether it is about ensuring that members of the team who are extroverted or introverted feel that they have a voice.

Leading by example is a powerful form of social nudging, where desired behaviours are modelled, subtly encouraging others to adopt them. As a manager, you set the tone for your team and build an inclusive environment.

Being supportive

Being supportive means: providing positive reinforcement, celebrating achievements, facilitating development opportunities, and offering guidance as Sarah explains:

> You have to empathise, understand, trust, empower.

Treat all members with equal respect and apply policies consistently across the board. Acknowledge your own limitations, practice active listening, and show genuine concern for employee wellbeing. Be humble and always admit your mistakes to your own manager. Manage your own emotions effectively and respond to others with empathy and understanding. Implementing these practices requires ongoing effort and commitment.

Treating everyone the same is not the solution. Mehmet considers the different approach needed for each team member:

> One of my directors said line management is the hardest thing to do because you have to be a different person to different people. And that's very true because all of your direct reports or all the people you're working with have different requirements. Some people might need a little bit of extra support, they might need more direction, others will run away and take things and bring back something fantastic or something that needs a bit more refining. The skill is trying to recognise what everyone needs out of you. If someone needs support at the beginning, you can give them that support and then let them run away, and that's fantastic. If there's something that you need to refine later, you can plan that as well. But then some people just need support throughout and need a bit of motivating to believe in themselves, think about or see things differently.

Credibility

Credibility is essential for a manager because it fosters trust, respect, and cooperation. It comes from having good management manners. You need to have mechanisms in place to know that your approach is working. If you are too hands-off and suddenly find out that there has been an operational disaster that you weren't aware of, you must take responsibility for it.

David D. sums up the principles with an example from his experience:

> I think that being open is key because as soon as you talk rubbish, you get tripped up and you have got to start from scratch with credibility.

If you're open and you overshare a little bit or if you say something that makes someone doubt you, you can come back from that more easily, I think. Starting the team, working out our remit, learning that whole thing together was energising and challenging in equal measure. I was managing two specialists, and happily, one was a specialist on systems, one was a specialist on research finance. So I could say, well, why don't you train each other, and I'll sit in and also benefit from your knowledge? And I was quite open about it, and I think that's really key for credibility.

Empowerment

Jeanette draws on her experience of competitive handball (as a player and coach) to share her vision of an empowered confident team:

> I often think about this when I do my management or coaching, how these are so similar to team sports. You have a team, and if you put the right people together, you have everyone's skills, their strengths and weaknesses, so you put them in the right position to ultimately score and win. Sorry for the cliche metaphor here, but it really is like that. And you have the coach. The leader isn't necessarily telling the team what to do, but they prepare them along the way to reach that goal and how to score and win.

Empowering your team members is about giving them autonomy, encouraging collaboration, and providing opportunities for innovation and professional development. It involves trust and support from you.

We can be cautious in protecting our team and wanting to control the narrative with senior colleagues. David F. explains that this should never prevent us from creating an empowering, supportive environment:

> I think a lot of people get really anxious about the control aspect of feeling that, as the manager, you should deliver information to senior management. I remember a particular occasion where a team member had worked really hard with me on getting to grips with designing emails and learning how they had to be built and all of the elements needed. She'd built them all. And we're doing an internal presentation of a campaign and I remember having a conversation with my manager and saying that my team member was going to talk about the email bit. And my manager said, 'No, you need to talk about it.' And I replied, 'Well, they built them, they should talk about them.' They've lived and breathed them. They know them better than I do, why would I talk about them? I think it's breaking down those barriers that, yes, there are big things that you do need to go and take care of to support the team, to protect the team, to communicate upwards, but also you can enable the team to communicate without feeling like you're crushing that completely.

Trust

Joanne explains how empowerment is only possible with trust:

> I moved into a role three months ago with a big team from very different areas. And I'm now confident in the sense that, I don't know the details of everyone's roles and I'm never going to know the ins and outs, but I know that each person is good at their job. We'll have one-to-ones, we'll talk about things, but actually, the day to day, that's their responsibility. And I think I'm now confident in the fact that I don't need to know everything. And I think when you're starting out, you think you do and that's when you micromanage. I've got a broad understanding, but I think when you feel like you need to know everything so you can assess whether people are doing a good job, that then becomes overbearing.

I prefer to trust first and only withdraw privileges if someone abuses that trust, rather than expect professional team members to have to earn my trust. I also feel strongly that as a manager, I must demonstrate my trustworthiness to my team members. Why should they blindly accept what I say when we first start working together? They need to see my abilities and potential impact in action.

Sarah finds negative discourses about colleagues – particularly junior staff – working from home frustrating:

> There's mistrust in some organisations of anybody working at home. They thought that administrators were doing nothing during COVID lockdowns because they weren't doing face-to-face work like teaching, when in actual fact they were doing so much more than they'd ever done before, and in fact having breakdowns at home from so much work. Of course, there are always people that are not as trustworthy but unless somebody's taking advantage on a regular basis then I'm happy to give and take with people. If they want to leave early, I know they're going to come back and get the work done because they feel they're in an environment where they're trusted to get on with it. Generally, we don't see them abusing that trust.

Confidentiality and discretion are essential. Your team will not trust you if you engage in office politics or share information given in confidence. When I was in school, I once reported some of my classmates for messing about with aerosols and lighters. The teacher told my classmates that I had reported them, and they unleashed their wrath on me. I never want anyone to be in that position as a result of something I have let slip.

Delegation

When I first started as a manager, I didn't used to be very good at delegating. I would get frustrated explaining tasks to others and waiting for them to complete them. It seemed easier just to do such tasks myself. It might feel easier or quicker in the moment, but in the long term, it's definitely not easier to take on such jobs yourself. You have to put in some time and make a commitment to empower and train your team so that they are confident taking on the tasks that you might share. In the long term, you're going to gain time because the team member is going to be able to succeed in the tasks you delegate to them. They're going to gain confidence, experience, and knowledge. So next time you think that it would be easier if you do the task yourself, just take a pause. See if you can find the time to work on delegating well.

Here are five principles that have helped me to delegate successfully and constructively:

1 Choose someone with appropriate skills, experience, and availability for each task.
2 Provide clear instructions and expectations to ensure that the person understands the task and their role.
3 Set realistic expectations and deadlines and ensure the result is measurable to avoid confusion and stress.
4 Check in and offer feedback at agreed intervals.
5 Restrain yourself when you feel the need to interfere! If you hate being micromanaged, so do your team members.

It is important to remember that as a manager you have a different role to your team members. You should not be doing the same work as them. Your responsibility is to support and facilitate their successful completion of their work.

It's not a good idea to take everything on yourself and become what is often referred to as a 'single point of failure'. If you do this, when you are not there everything could grind to a halt. Peter learnt from experience the damage this can do:

> I did everything myself and I was really passionate about what I did. Then I left and – I'm blaming myself rather than giving myself credit – everything fell apart because nobody had any idea what was going on. It was a massive mistake to do everything myself. So now I try to ensure a team approach, so if I'm not there, others know what the situation is, whoever you're dealing with knows those people and so you have that safeguard in place. I know from experience that if you become that one person, it's fine in the short term but the long-term success of the organisation isn't great.

You are not your team's search engine

It is amusing how irritated we, as professionals in higher education, can get with applicants, academics, and students and their seemingly simple enquiries. We might think: 'Why didn't they just google it? Surely it was harder for them to find our phone number and call us to ask about it than it would have been to just google the question?' Or the classic, usually from an applicant or student, 'Nobody told me to do x!' Our internal voice might respond with: 'Well, yes, but no one told you to call us to complain about it either, so how have you managed that?' We are all guilty of being selective as to when we take initiative!

When team members try to use me as their search engine, I don't answer their questions with the quick answer they are after. To empower your team so that they feel confident finding information for themselves and so they take initiative to enhance their own knowledge, ask questions of your own:

What are you trying to find out?
What challenges are you facing?
What things have you tried to do to resolve this problem so far?
How far have you got with your assessment of this challenge against the criteria or process that we're using?
How can I help you find a resolution to this query?

It might seem easier sometimes to just answer the question. And, yes, sometimes you might need to know where there is a knowledge gap. But doing this all the time doesn't work in the long term nor does it create a culture of taking initiative or responsibility. How you manage your team affects how they grow and develop. Always giving solutions rather than helping someone work out their own solutions, creates dependency, reliance, and passivity. I think we all want team members who take initiative, make the best use of resources, and feel confident.

Confidence

Most of us have a conception of what being a 'good' manager might look like and what we could and/or should do to be that person. But fear and lack of confidence can hold us back. We might stick with what is comfortable, with the status quo, with what we know from our own managers is accepted and expected in our workplace. Jenny found it inhibiting:

> I didn't like managing people because of my lack of confidence in my own abilities. I always think that the person that I'm managing could do better than me. I probably need to work on that!

David F. reminds us to temper our expectations:

> Don't seek validation elsewhere because it doesn't always come, people don't always see it. Think about the people you care about at work and the opinions that they have, and they're the people that will probably come

back and say: 'Thank you for doing that. That was really helpful.' They're the people that matter. I think celebrating those wins and those learning opportunities and growing and moving forward from it is really important.

Jeanette shares her strategy for countering the self-critical feelings we all battle with:

> I learned some key things. For instance, it's about resetting how you talk to yourself, the negative speak, negative thinking, particularly when things are not going well. So that could be, 'I'm not doing what I'm meant to be doing, I'm rubbish, I'm bad, I'm not as good as I think I am.' And there you go down the spiral. Or you're not having a good time at work because your manager is criticising you or you're not getting the praise that you think you're going to get. And again, the bad talk is starting. We can be quite hard, I think, when we talk to ourselves. We would never speak to anyone else the way we talk to ourselves. Instead, visualise yourself achieving, scoring, performing, etc. I go back to the stuff I know and remembering my skills and abilities and everything I do. And if your mind thinks you can do it, I mean, you're halfway there, aren't you? We all have self-doubt. So then I go, 'Right, I have all these skills and abilities, I am really good' and I can get out of bad thinking and move on. I think this is really important because if you let the bad thinking fester, that and the self-talk, is just negative. You are then on a very slippery slope.

Peer support

The support of others in management roles is invaluable for building your confidence and developing your professional practice. David D. highlights the solidarity in the unique uncertainties of working in higher education management that he feels as a line manager:

> There's a sense of unification with other managers and other people in the profession because there isn't a rulebook. Our institution has grappled for years with what management training could or should look like and there have been several false dawns. I don't know what answer we'll ever find, and I don't know what will ever be consistently applicable across professional managers, let alone professional and academic ones.

Joanne regularly draws on her long-standing network of colleagues for support and advice:

> There was a number of us all on the same level and that was really useful because you had that peer-to-peer support, and we could talk about problems. I think it's really difficult to manage alone. And I know when I started

over twenty years ago, mentoring and coaching wasn't really a big thing. But now I've had a mentor and I've mentored people, coming into management it's really important to have support, whether it's coaching, mentoring or having that peer support, or just somebody who you can bounce ideas off. And I still do it now. I'm still really good friends with a manager in a different school, even though I've had three different roles since then. I rang him the other day and said, 'Right, I've got this challenge.' Sometimes you just need somebody to talk to about challenges. And I think we don't offer that enough. Sometimes in the sector we just make assumptions that people can manage.

Managing former peers

Securing a role that means managing former peers is an added challenge.

Acknowledge the change and make a conscious effort to step into your new role as if you were new to the team altogether. You will need to move away from a peer relationship to a manager/employee relationship. It is often discomfiting for all parties. David D. found it challenging to make this shift:

> I was very driven at the beginning by the desire to be the line manager I always wanted to have. I don't feel that I want to distance myself from anything I did in that first role, but it very much felt like I was trying to lead among peers, and I was probably trying to be their friend as much as anything else.

You will never know all the answers

Sarah sums it up neatly:

> This world isn't black and white. This is actually quite a grey kind of environment because it's always changing. Don't worry that you might not always know the answer, because the answer isn't always there.

People management is hard. Be kind to yourself. Before I worked with an excellent manager, I had very difficult relationships with most of my managers. That experience allowed me to set more realistic expectations for myself as a manager. I knew that I didn't need to be perfect. If I had always had excellent managers, I might have felt the need to be perfect. I wanted not to be a 'bad' manager. To achieve that, I focused on consistency and transparency. My aim was to be an imperfect manager who learns from their mistakes, is clear in communication with their team, is consistent, and is fair. That is my idea of a 'good' manager. I want to be imperfect yet continuously working towards self-awareness, self-improvement, and better professional practice. You will feel uncomfortable at times. So cut yourself some slack and be kind to yourself.

Digging deeper

What are your goals for leading your team? How will you measure your progress and success?

How will you cultivate an inclusive environment that values diversity and encourages participation from all team members?

How will you identify opportunities to delegate tasks appropriately and empower your team members to take ownership? Are there areas where you might be reluctant to delegate? Why?

Read: Starr, J., 2023. *Brilliant coaching*, 4th ed. Harlow: Pearson Education Limited. This is a comprehensive introduction to using coaching conversations as a manager. Lots of practical exercises and tips.

Enrol: OpenLearn free online course: Managing and managing people. Available at: www.open.edu/openlearn/money-business/leadership-management/managing-and-managing-people.

Review: Equality, diversity and inclusion (EDI) in the workplace factsheet, CIPD. Available at: www.cipd.org/uk/knowledge/factsheets/diversity-factsheet.

References

CAST, 2024. The UDL guidelines. *CAST*. Available at: <https://udlguidelines.cast.org/>.

Dunbar, D., 2014. Communication – putting the manners (back) into management. *Perspectives: Policy and Practice in Higher Education*, 18(3), pp. 84–89. https://doi.org/10.1080/13603108.2014.938138.

Harwood, V., Hickey-Moody, A., McMahon, S. and O'Shea, S., 2017. *The politics of widening participation and university access for young people: making educational futures*. London: Routledge.

Lawrence, T. B. and Corwin, V., 2023. Being there: the acceptance and marginalization of part-time professional employees. *Journal of Organizational Behavior*, 24(8), pp. 923–943. https://doi.org/10.1002/job.229.

Chapter 6

Adapt, advocate, advance
Embracing change and innovation

The world of higher education is a dynamic one, constantly evolving with new policies, technological advancements, and strategic shifts. This chapter equips you to ride this wave of change with confidence. It highlights the importance of staying informed, emphasising how staying abreast of these developments empowers you to navigate uncertainty and contribute meaningfully.

Understanding your institution's unique culture is key to influencing change strategically. This chapter provides practical tips on staying informed. It moves beyond simply keeping up – you'll learn how to take ownership of change, collaborate effectively with your team, and leverage frameworks for clear communication and successful implementation. This proactive approach ensures you're not just weathering the storm, but actively shaping a brighter future for your institution.

Sector-wide change

The unpredictable, yet continuous nature of change in policy is characteristic of higher education. New or re-purposed technology, strategy and policy; innovations and initiatives; rollbacks and revisions – change is an opportunity to learn, grow, and explore. It can also be frustrating. A successful career in higher education, as Sarah says, requires resilience:

> You do need to be very adaptable to the external changes.

You might be happy where you are, in your current role. However, the world around you keeps moving. You will change. Your team will change. The expectations you have of yourself and others have of you will shift over time. What it means to do your job well will evolve.

What drives change?

There are many complex factors driving and shaping change in the UK higher education sector, including funding pressures, regulatory changes, and technological advancements.

UK HEIs are battling a continued decline in public funding (undergraduate home fees have been frozen since 2017), leading them to seek alternative revenue streams and explore cost-saving measures. This impacts professional services by demanding greater efficiency, requiring them to explore income generation strategies and potentially leading to job cuts or restructuring. International recruitment has been a significant focus for income generation, but that is vulnerable to changes to government policy (such as the 2024 restrictions on students bringing dependents which significantly impacted recruitment numbers).

The UK government has implemented various policies and regulations which impact higher education, such as the Teaching Excellence Framework (TEF) and Office for Students (OfS) regulations. These changes necessitate adjustments in areas like quality assurance, compliance, and data management, affecting professional services involved in these functions.

The rise of online learning platforms and blended learning models, combining online and on-campus elements, requires HEIs to adapt teaching methods, invest in technology infrastructure, and potentially restructure administrative processes. This might impact professional services in areas like learning technology support, curriculum development, and student recruitment and engagement.

As technology plays a more prominent role in higher education, ethical concerns regarding data privacy, intellectual property, AI, and online content moderation require careful attention. HEIs may need to update policies and procedures to ensure ethical practices and compliance with relevant regulations.

Why keep up to date?

Why is it important you keep up to date with developments across the sector and in your discipline? You might have the mindset that if it's that important then someone more senior than you will let you know about it. So you might think, why worry until you are told to worry. Are you sure that is a good idea? Will your senior managers understand the granular impact of a change or new strategy? Will they be aware of or engage with government consultation appropriately? Do you want to be always on the back foot reacting to something instead of leading from the front?

As I have said before, I work in admissions. In my department, we knew there would be amendments to the fee regulations regarding access to funding for EU nationals. But what would they be? When might they be implemented? This was definitely not very high up the government's list of concerns or priorities. Until the draft amendments to the fee regulations were published in February 2021 (and adopted into law in March 2021), admissions teams across England had to consider how to support EU applicants from the opening of the University and Colleges Admissions Service (UCAS) application cycle in September 2020, without any official guidance.

We submitted a proposal to senior management for consideration and implementation before the start of the application cycle. Unfortunately, as was the case in many HEIs, uncertainty around predicting the potential outcome of the government's decision on fee eligibility of EU nationals, and a focus on the potential financial impact of the COVID-19 pandemic, inhibited decision-making.

Decision-paralysis can be a characteristic of one model of institutional leadership in higher education. The ambiguity (or contingency) model is demonstrated by a lack of clarity around organisational goals and processes, a fragmentation of institutional structure, a prevalence of unplanned decisions, and a dependence on external bodies for direction (Bush, 2020).

As officers and managers on the ground, we are rarely able to directly influence decision-making at a senior and strategic level. But we can be ready with answers and a plan. In the scenario above with my team, we did have a plan. The proposal, that my manager and I had drafted before the cycle, which included a detailed operational plan, was ready to be implemented at the point that senior leaders finally recognised the need for it. Therefore, we were able to move fast and ensure that the adopted strategy was fit for purpose straight away.

How to keep up to date with developments

The best way to keep up to date with changes in policy is to read, watch, or listen to the news regularly. I find too much news difficult to process and it can fuel my anxiety, so I carefully manage how I engage with it. I review online news sites weekly reading any articles relating to higher education that might be relevant, such as changes to the health sector that might impact health education. Your choice of news site is up to you – but consider the rigour of the journalism and its political affiliations.

Subscribe to – and actually *read* – sector or discipline mailing lists. Wonkhe is an excellent digestible, sector-wide newsletter. At least if you subscribe, it will drop into your inbox every week and you will read it when you have the time and inclination.

Seek opportunities to engage with colleagues or organisation across the sector. For example, UCAS hold regional forums that recruitment and admissions colleagues can attend to keep abreast of developments.

What impact are sector changes having on professional services?

Sector changes in higher education are impacting professional services in a multitude of ways. Here are just a few.

As technology advances, repetitive administrative tasks are increasingly automated, which can lead to job losses or changes in responsibilities for professional services staff. HEIs might consolidate certain services across departments to improve efficiency and save costs, impacting staffing structures and workflows within professional services. Due to funding pressures, HEIs may need to operate with fewer resources, requiring professional services teams to adopt leaner operating models and work more efficiently.

HEIs are increasingly utilising data to inform decision-making. This demands new skills and expertise within professional services for data analysis, reporting, and translating data insights into actionable strategies. As reliance on technology increases, cybersecurity becomes paramount. Professional services might need to develop expertise in data security protocols, risk management, and user education to protect sensitive information.

HEIs are placing greater emphasis on the overall student experience, necessitating collaboration between professional services and academic departments to provide holistic support and to cater to diverse student needs. This might involve developing new services, streamlining administrative processes, and enhancing communication channels.

Students expect personalised learning experiences (and timetables!) and access to tailored support services. This may require the development of flexible learning pathways, more personalised tutor support, and the evolution of more adaptable student support systems.

The move towards lifelong learning and degree apprenticeships necessitates the development of new programmes and services catered to working professionals and non-traditional students. This requires professional services to adapt marketing strategies, develop flexible learning models and create efficient enrolment, and support processes for these new student groups.

HEIs compete globally for students and research funding, necessitating professional services to develop effective internationalisation strategies. This might involve marketing, student recruitment, and managing partnerships with international institutions.

Innovation and influencing change locally

Often, higher education faces a paradox when it comes to change. While the sector operates in a dynamic environment, constantly adjusting to external forces, its response to these changes can be slow and reactive.

This contradiction can be attributed to several factors: bureaucracy, power dynamics, many stakeholders, and risk aversion.

HEIs are often characterised by complex hierarchical structures with numerous committees and decision-making bodies. While committees can play a crucial role in promoting collaboration and diverse perspectives, the excessive use of these groups can stifle innovation and lead to information silos, hindering clear communication and swift action. The division of authority within HEIs can be ambiguous, making it unclear who has the final say in implementing changes. This can lead to delays and frustration as proposals navigate various approval stages. Balancing the diverse interests of different stakeholders, such as faculty, staff, students, and administrators, can be challenging. This can lead to resistance to change and protracted negotiation processes. The inherent risk-averse nature of some institutions may lead to a preference for maintaining the status quo over embracing innovative solutions, even when faced with compelling evidence for change.

David F. finds it frustrating:

> I still struggle with the decision-making process, and I loathe being in a meeting where I don't have any actions unless it is a genuine update meeting. But I've never before been in more meetings that are meetings about meetings, and it's like, 'What do you want me to do because of it? What are my actions? Are we just all walking away? And we'll come back next week and chat about it again. How do we move this forward?'

HEIs are not known for their decision-making speed or detailed forward planning. There's usually a strategic plan, and many other plans that feed into it (such as the Access and Participation Plan), but how much gets done and how much risk is taken depends on the individual institution – its leadership model and its appetite for risk – and what external change the government has thrown at it that year.

There are a few different models of leadership in operation at institutions across the sector. For example, the model of distributed leadership focuses on collaborative decision-making that recognises and enables the specialist skills and knowledge of its members (Bush, 2020). This model supports responsive and reactive decision-making, recognising expertise and investing organisational confidence in decisions. The formal or bureaucratic model is characterised by a strict hierarchy, directive management, a focus on process, and a 'top-down' decision-making style (Bush, 2020). The collegial model is characterised by setting clear goals, fostering intellectual growth, leading by example with key values, setting ambitious standards, cultivating a positive environment, and establishing inclusive structures for involvement in decision-making (Leithwood, 1994). Understanding the characteristics of your organisation's institutional and operational leadership models and culture is crucial to finding ways for you to manage, initiate and mitigate change.

Understanding the complex interplay of factors contributing to the slow pace of change in higher education is crucial for navigating the challenging landscape. While the environment may be constantly in flux, overcoming bureaucratic hurdles, fostering collaboration and finding ways to work within the system are vital to driving positive change within HEIs. You will need a strategy.

Strategies for influencing change

Change in higher education can tend towards a focus on the technical rather than culture: delivering projects within a silo rather than deploying projects to facilitate structural, cultural, and institutional change or development. A project delivered in isolation with limited buy-in from staff and no contextual structural change can only have limited success.

An example springs to mind of a new self-service tool that was developed and deployed for academic staff to use. Training on how to use the functionality was limited as the project team considered it quite straightforward to use. Academic colleagues did not appreciate having to self-serve on something that previously an administrator had sent them individually by email. Unsurprisingly, there was resistance and frustration on all sides. 'Why do I have to do this extra work?' versus 'Why won't the academics use this simple tool we built them?'

Most change models and frameworks assume change leadership from the top. This is great in one respect, but an important question is: how can we, on the ground, with our limited influence and opportunity in our areas of responsibility innovate and facilitate progressive change?

Magda shares her advice on how to present changes to others:

> Nobody really gets stuck in the old ways too long because things change really quickly of their own accord anyway and people are just so used to embracing change and making the most of it. You don't get a lot of resistance here, especially if you're able to justify what you're trying to achieve, come really prepared and bring evidence to prove that it is going to make a difference. Really believe in what you're saying and be honest with people. Be direct with them. It just works. It also helps that I enjoy change and adapt really quickly. And I'm also quite resilient so I don't take things personally as a rule. I've learned that even if someone gets upset with what I'm trying to achieve or change and they don't want to collaborate, they're really upset with the situation. They're not upset with me. So I don't take things personally.

Here are the key elements for achieving change:

Evidence: Support your ideas with data, research, case studies, customer feedback, and so forth, showing an evidential need for change and the potential risks of maintaining the status quo. David F. deploys an evidenced-based approach:

> How do we change some things, and how do we get buy in for that change? I think that starts at a small level with testing and with proof. What does the data say to begin with? So I always start with analytics.

Network: Build relationships with colleagues, supervisors, and other stakeholders who might be receptive to your ideas. If you can get a senior leader on your side, doors will open.

Focus on achievable goals: Start with small, manageable changes that are likely to succeed and demonstrate the value of your ideas.

Define measurements of success: Ensure that you integrate mechanisms to monitor and demonstrate impact, output, and benefits.

Pilot your concept: Implement your ideas in a limited way to gather feedback and refine your approach, as Magda prefers to:

> Usually if you say, 'Okay, let's try it for a month', people are more willing to bend and act in a more flexible manner because they are like, 'Okay, fine, after a few weeks, we'll be able to go back to the old ways.' But then very often during the trial they get an epiphany that, actually, maybe this new way is better. So very often I'll get them to switch perspective through that pilot.

Celebrate successes: Share your wins, big and small, to build enthusiasm and encourage others to get involved.

Be collaborative and build alliances: Look for others who share your concerns and seek their support. Show genuine interest in understanding their perspectives and concerns. Focus on shared goals and values to build consensus and collaboration.

Communicate effectively: Articulate your message clearly and focus on the benefits of change, with evidence to support it, adapting your communication style to your audience and their needs. Senior leaders usually want headlines whereas operational staff want to know how they will be directly impacted.

Identify existing resources: Look for policies, initiatives, or budgets that can support your change efforts. Use established channels of communication to voice your ideas. Simon considers:

> In terms of what is achievable, who do we need to help us get there?

Change takes time and persistence. Being patient, adaptable, and willing to learn from setbacks are invaluable skills to prevent frustration winning out. Sarah reminds us we are capable:

> You've got an enquiring mind, you've got tenacity and you're willing to find a solution.

Continuous improvement

Change is not often a big bang event. Likely you will be mostly focused on continuous improvement and incremental change over time. Magda enjoys the challenge:

> I keep reviewing processes and procedures. It's like a game, almost, of trying to see what else I can streamline, what else can I get rid of. Is there anything redundant here that I can either automate or merge or just make easy

for me, easy for my colleagues, easy for the students, easy for everyone? It's really worth having someone really lazy take a look at it as well because they will always find the easiest possible way around the issue because they can't be bothered to spend hours on something if they know there's a shortcut to be found. This continuous improvement path, for some reason, never gets boring.

Let's just say I'm one of those lazy people who embrace efficiency, perhaps to a fault. This talent for streamlining processes first showed itself in my very first job out of university. I started as an administrative assistant, and one of my early tasks was collating papers for a Planning Committee meeting. It involved adding the relevant agenda reference to the top of each application and its supporting documents. I tackled it head-on, adding the references directly to the PDFs and emailing them to the print room.

A few hours later, my supervisor approached me, a hint of worry etched on their face. The print deadline was looming, and they hadn't seen me hunched over the copier or lugging a stack of papers around. Confused, I explained my streamlined approach – the PDFs were already marked up and on their way.

My supervisor's jaw nearly hit the floor. Apparently, the usual process involved printing everything out, creating a separate list with reference codes, then manually cutting out and sticking those codes onto the physical documents! Needless to say, that tradition ended that day.

Don't underestimate the importance of adaptability and navigating existing structures. Rather than waiting for drastic reform, workarounds and improvements within the current system can sometimes be found. This may involve identifying champions for change, building coalitions across different departments and leveraging existing resources to implement small but impactful changes. Network is vital, as Julie explains:

> Don't just treat your changes as projects, as transactions, which you need to complete before you move on to the next thing. Really think about how you can nurture that network. Most projects are achieved through leveraging where resources and expertise are throughout the organisation and by leveraging the good relationships that you have with other people. In a resource-constrained environment, where quite often, the space, time or human resource isn't there, it's goodwill that makes these things happen.

Supporting your team through change

In terms of change management, empathy and open-mindedness are key for senior leaders, who should advocate for change aligned with strategic goals. Middle managers and team leaders bridge communication and drive change initiatives, empowering their teams towards positive outcomes. It can be hard, as David F. observes:

> I think HE's a sector that regularly gets rocked by all kinds of different things and staying upbeat when resource is an issue, budgets are an issue and government's an issue, is hard. All of these things are outside of your control.

There are strategies you can use to support your team through change and manage reluctance and anxiety amongst team members relating to change.

Communication and engagement

Julie is an experienced change leader and project manager. She shares her top ten strategies for effectively communicating change and engaging stakeholders:

1 Stay on brand, establish your key messages, and use those to ensure clear messaging.
2 Communicate the 'why' and 'what' the change means to stakeholders to remove threat and fear.
3 Provide a range of engagement mechanisms to cater to different learning and personality styles and timelines.
4 Create different forums for stakeholders to engage with, contribute to and feel ownership of so they feel an active part of the change.
5 Refine communication strategies to make the picture clear and understand the necessary actions for course correction.
6 Communicate benefits and successes widely, as early as possible, and frequently.
7 Build internal networks and trusted relationships to leverage change.
8 Balance people and outcomes when approaching change management.
9 Use an engagement-led approach to gather feedback from stakeholders and adjust approaches accordingly.
10 Leverage observations about how change feels for recipients to inform sponsors and senior leaders.

She draws a clear distinction between communication and engagement:

> Communication is outward. It's broadcast, for want of a better expression. Engagement is a two-way mechanism. The perfect blend for me is having that communication and engagement side by side. This is because the engagement allows you to check that the understanding is there, but it also allows you that temperature check on the cultural elements in terms of what's landing well and what's not landing well. It also gives the opportunity for people to feel that they have an active role in shaping the future. An engagement point allows people to come to the table, bring suggestions,

and build what the future is. That's very different to being told what the future is. So if you can marry up engagement and communication together, that's quite powerful.

Her advice is to vary communication and engagement methods for maximum impact:

> This is part of the layering that you need to think about. There are written comms: 'I've put it on teams', 'I've sent it in an email' or 'I've mentioned it at a meeting'. How else can you layer it? Are there team and department days or meetings away days, staff, networks, newsletters, intranets? Keep layering your key messages because different audiences will pick up on those channels. It's better to make use of all of those channels and then people can self-select how they choose to consume it. It's an art and different things work in different environments, so it takes a bit of it takes trial and error.

It might seem as though you are constantly repeating yourself, but this is important, as Julie explains:

> When you give the briefing, in whatever form it is, you have an immediate opportunity for questions. Good practice is to then provide some kind of online forum or mechanism for people to be able to put their questions in, which picks up your reflectors and people that might feel more comfortable posting anonymously. And then you have the conversation again in two- or three-weeks' time.
> Yes, it might feel tiring, and yes, it might feel like you're going over old ground, but it means that those that haven't spoken up at the start, or those that are of the personality type that find it hard to speak up have a chance to come back to it and engage. So for me, it's about having a series of engagement points to continue for people to be able to ask questions and to continue the dialogue. One discussion at the beginning is not going to cut it.

Resistance to change

People often resist change, whether it's that the introduction of a self-service tool or a process change. Some fear losing control, while others struggle with uncertainty or the disruption to their routines. Anxiety about additional workload and memories of past resentments or challenges can flare up. Surprises and drastic changes can be particularly off-putting, as can feeling unprepared or unsupported. People like to be experts in their particular areas. Something new or different can feel uncomfortable (Moss Kanter, 2012). David D. advises creating space for team members to voice their concerns:

> You don't owe loyalty to a process or to a service. You owe loyalty to your sense of professional identity and the people around you. And sometimes

you need to let people vent and let off some steam, and sometimes you need to say, 'I hear what you're saying', and then bring a bit of perspective to the conversation. And that can be hard to do.

Julie agrees that working out the root cause of the change resistance is crucial to addressing it:

It sounds really simplistic, but reaching out for a chat with someone to find out where the resistance is coming from normally goes a long way. You don't show up to the conversation and ask, 'Why are you not cooperating with this change?' You show up to the conversation and say, 'I'm interested in hearing your experience about how this is going for you' or 'How do you feel about this?' It's about a conversation with the individual and really listening to what comes up. Sometimes what they say the first time isn't actually what's going on at all. You have to dig underneath a couple of layers to get to their real feelings or the real source of resistance. Sometimes it's going to take you two, three, four conversations to get to that point. So don't expect that you're going to have a 20-minute conversation and, voilà, it's all sorted. Unpicking change resistance can take an investment of time building up trusted relationships but can also pay dividends.

Addressing these concerns means creating a sense of safety and ownership. Encourage participation in planning, provide clear communication, and focus on essential changes rather than unnecessary disruptions. Change overload and poor timing can be a barrier to positive engagement, as Julie explains:

Some of the resistance is about all of the things that happen in an academic calendar and lots of initiatives at the same time. Can you realistically defer elements of your change until that pressure has eased? Can you be much more sympathetic about your project and your pacing? Can you do a more iterative rollout, which means that you've got fewer resource demands? Or do you need to have a conversation upwards about volume of workloads? You're not actually going to know that until you've had a conversation to explore it and understand the position on the ground.

Offer training and support to address skill concerns and ease transitions. Acknowledge the challenges of change and offer recognition to those involved. Joanne considers the scale of change and its potential impact:

Systems change. Everybody rolls their eyes, but they do the training, and they get it to work and then they're like, 'Actually, we quite like it!' But I think when it's structural change and it's impacting your role, and that's when people get a little bit defensive and a little bit scared. And I think that's where it's gone wrong before. So it's very much about getting them to engage: 'This is what's going to happen. This is what we're expecting of you. This is what the structure will look like.' And I think most of the time when people hear the word change, it's always fear for their jobs. If it is the case, however you do it, you just need to communicate with them from the start and give them space to ask questions and give them space to rant if they need. I think we put on staff so much in terms of, 'This is what we're doing' without that consultation. And even if the decision has been made, at least let them feel like they've had a voice in it sometimes just to say, 'We are making the change, but let's hear what you think.'

Magda emphasises framing change in a positive light:

> I try to be excited and really believe in the change that I'm trying to achieve in the first place. I need to believe that it's going to make a difference.

Change coming from the top

Effective change communication hinges on a range of factors, including clarity of vision, participation, action plan, resistance management, and recognition. Change often comes from the top, however we can't always rely on our leaders and our organisation to manage change well. As managers, we have a vital role in supporting our teams. There are lots of frameworks and tools to help us. This five-step framework from Workleap (2021) helps ensure we cover all the steps towards change and take a structured approach:

1 **Paint a clear picture of the 'why'** behind the change, connecting it to the bigger picture and organisational values. This provides context and motivates buy-in.
2 Don't just lecture; **open the floor for questions, concerns, and feedback**. This fosters a sense of ownership and community.
3 **Share the plan** with next steps to ease anxieties and encourage progress. Be transparent and offer as much clarity as possible, but don't overload with information. Co-creation of some operational details of the plan (adjusting it based on feedback) where possible is valuable for ensuring joint ownership of the change.
4 **Expect and address resistance** through individual conversations. Recognise and understand the fear behind that resistance and address those concerns directly.
5 **Celebrate small wins** to boost morale and positivity during the transition.

Effective communication requires planning, clear messaging, and a safe space for honest discussion. David D. explains how this can build resilience within a team:

> I think that at a fundamental level, there are two types of how to do things. One of them is related to what you bring to a role, a service, an activity,

a process. And the other is related to the way that you work on your computer or in your systems. I think if you feel comfortable with your personal 'how', so 'I'm going to approach this process with empathy, with efficiency' and 'I'm going to try and make sure that the student voice is included' and if you feel comfortable with that and you're less attached to the actual process itself, I think that can help. Giving people the space and the permission to find their professional identity can really help them be more resilient to change because there is something about them that will be a constant.

By embracing these principles, you can navigate change smoothly and empower your team to thrive. Joanne reflects on the strategies that she has learnt that can be problematic:

I don't do this now, but there were times when I was new in my career that I'd say, 'You know what, I don't want to do this, but I've been asked to do it and I've been asked to tell you that we've got to do it.' And in hindsight now, I realise that that's not the way to do it. And it's taken me a while to say that, for me. I am selling why we're doing it. If it's statutory, great, and you can say it's statutory. But if it's come from a senior manager and I don't agree with it, my job is to sell it like I do agree with it, even if I don't. Then I have to answer the difficult questions and say, well, let's have a conversation about it. But I don't think putting it on somebody else, if it is just a request and not something that we have to do for various reasons, is particularly healthy. But sometimes it's really difficult not to say, 'Do you know what? I agree with you, but we've just got to do it.'

I sometimes wish I could tell my team that the proposal on the table is 100 times better than the crazy thing that was first suggested. Alas, we must be diplomatic!

Encouraging your team to engage in opportunities

Encourage your team to engage in projects so they feel more ownership of change. Don't wait for staff to express interest – actively seek out opportunities that stretch their skills and expose them to new areas. This could involve assigning them tasks outside their comfort zone, encouraging participation in projects and events, or nominating them for training opportunities. Help your team members set SMART goals that align with their aspirations and the HEI's needs. These goals should encourage proactive behaviour, such as taking on new challenges or developing specific skills.

Simon pushes his team members to get involved and articulates the benefits of doing so:

There's a really big, university-wide project currently ongoing so I will always be trying to sell it to my team. I'll say, 'If you've got the capacity, be involved, because that's the best way that you can affect change. You've told me that this hurts and that you're spending ages on this, so this genuinely is your opportunity to have influence.' It's not about being visible and seen, it's about genuinely having that opportunity to improve things and make them better.

Recognising and celebrating success will encourage team members to get involved in future initiatives. Julie advises:

> Communicate your benefits and successes widely. People are quite quiet about that. You find these wonderful projects and they've produced all this fantastic stuff, yet they don't talk about it. So find a mechanism to be able to share successes and celebrate them, and that will make your people that worked on the project feel 100 per cent better.

None of this will work unless you lead by example and demonstrate proactiveness yourself. Take on new challenges, volunteer for projects, and continuously seek learning opportunities.

Digging deeper

How will you stay informed about policy updates, technology advancements, and strategic shifts in higher education? What are your preferred sources of information?

How can you effectively collaborate with colleagues from different departments and disciplines to navigate change together?

Identify a specific change happening in your institution: How can you apply the information from this chapter to understand it better and prepare for its impact?

Read: HEPI, 2023. How universities should design change initiatives for success. *HEPI*. Available at: https://www.hepi.ac.uk/wp-content/uploads/2023/11/Change-by-Design-How-universities-should-design-change-initiatives-for-success.pdf.

Sign up: Keep up to date with developments and debates by signing up to Wonkhe's popular email mailing list. There is also a podcast. Available at: https://wonkhe.com/.

Explore: There is a community of practice within Higher Education focusing on Lean and Improvement practice, which is helpful if you have an interest in how you might improve your processes and ways of working in your HEI, and the approaches which you might use to do this. The website (with links to the LinkedIn group and You Tube channel) is https://www.leanhe.org and you can also sign up for the Lean HE England mailing list at https://www.jiscmail.ac.uk.

References

Bush, T., 2020. *Theories of educational leadership and management*, 5th ed. London: SAGE.

Leithwood, K., 1994. Leadership for school restructuring. *Educational Administration Quarterly*, 30, pp. 498–518. https://doi.org/10.1177/0013161X94030004006.

Moss Kanter, R., 2012. Ten reasons people resist change. *Harvard Business Review*, 25 September. Available at: <https://hbr.org/2012/09/ten-reasons-people-resist-chang>.

Workleap, 2021. Leading through change: a 5-step framework. *Workleap*, 26 March. Available at: <https://workleap.com/blog/leading-through-change/>.

Chapter 7

Navigate, nurture, negotiate
Leading with confidence and tackling challenges

The transition from manager to leader in higher education marks a shift in focus. This chapter unpacks the multifaceted role of middle managers, distinguishing between the task-oriented nature of management and the visionary essence of leadership. It delves into the importance of authenticity and open communication as cornerstones of effective leadership.

The chapter works through some of the harder aspects of management, including navigating performance management, conflict resolution, and team emotions. Practical strategies are offered for tackling challenging situations like performance issues, emphasising the importance of early intervention, transparency, and support for team members.

Recognising the unique position of middle managers as mediators, negotiators, and relationship builders, this chapter aims to equip you with the tools to navigate challenges with diplomacy, fostering a collaborative and thriving team environment. Moving beyond theory, I and members of our community of practice share our personal philosophies on leadership and how those translate into tangible action.

What's the difference between management and leadership?

There is an extensive body of work and continuous debate about how management and leadership can be defined and the differences (and similarities) between the concepts. I'm not going to address that here. I just want to share two observations that help articulate useful ways to consider the terms in a professional context.

Management is a role. It is a job and a portfolio of responsibilities. It usually encompasses coordination, organisation, supervision and accountability for the creation, deployment, and use of resources (people, services, and things). It is about meeting targets, following policies, compliance, and delivering on the operational tasks.

Leadership is a concept. Bruce Peltier (2010) summed it up well when he said, 'Leadership is a lot like love. Everyone thinks it is special, but hardly anyone agrees on a definition'. We tend to think of it in terms of traits, competencies, skills, personality characteristics and that certain special something we can't define. It encompasses a strategic view. The skills of leadership – creative thinking, critical evaluation, problem-detection, communication, expectation-management skills, empowerment, and the confidence to challenge traditional ways of working – can be learnt (McCaffery, 2018).

Your leadership philosophy

There are many models and styles of leadership, from servant to authoritative, transactional to participative. I think developing and applying your own philosophy of leadership is the most effective way to 'do' people management. Managing and navigating people, resources, services, your own manager, politics, and many other challenges requires leadership skills. [For example, see John Kotter, *A Force for Change: How Leadership Differs from Management* (Cambridge: The Free Press, 1990).] Your ultimate goal is to deliver on your department's short- and long-term objectives. To do that you have to rely on others.

My own philosophy draws from what I've read, experienced, and observed. It's defined within a framework of my professional values: both my own internal values and the code of practice my discipline is committed to (in my case it is the Fair Admissions Code of Practice (UUK, 2023)).

I favour Peltier's articulation of leadership as innovation and change over more traditional concepts of leadership as high-level strategy (DiGirolamo & Tkach, 2019). My approach is focused on transparency, open communication, respect, advocacy, and empowerment. Overall, I strive for authenticity.

Authenticity

Authentic leadership has four key characteristics:

- 'self-awareness': being mindful of your strengths and weaknesses and working continuously to improve on them;
- 'internalised moral perspective': holding true to your own principles and values of leadership;
- 'balanced processing': fairness and consistency in decision-making and in how you deal with your team members, colleagues and customers; and
- 'relational transparency': saying what you mean, meaning what you say, and being honest and genuine (Walumbwa et al., 2008).

There are a lot of different interpretations of what authenticity might mean to leadership and what an authentic leader is. Ultimately, remember that most people will see straight through you if you're anything other than your true authentic self.

A senior staff member I knew of would repeatedly use the phrase 'real genuine thanks' in emails to express gratitude to operational teams. However, the insincerity of the phrase became obvious to everyone, as it was never followed by any concrete actions or genuine appreciation. The phrase quickly became an inside joke. If a manager thanked a team for something, someone would inevitably pipe up with, 'ah, but is it real *genuine* thanks?'

This story demonstrates the importance of alignment between words and actions in leadership. When you express gratitude through words but fail to follow up with actions that demonstrate genuine appreciation, it undermines the value of the words. This can have several negative consequences: erosion of trust, reduced motivation, and negative team culture. In contrast, when leaders demonstrate their appreciation through actions, they increase motivation, boost morale, and foster stronger relationships within the team.

As Magda cautions:

> You're not there to exploit the people who work for you, you're there to raise them up above you and just let them go. That takes work and commitment.

Sharing your struggles (strategically, of course!) humanises you and fosters empathy. It shows your team you understand their anxieties and can offer guidance based on your own experience. For example, when a team member confided in me about their anxiety, I was able to share some of the coping mechanisms that work for me. Their response? Relief. They appreciated having a leader who didn't just try to reassure them but offered practical strategies. There's a fear that vulnerability could be seen as weakness. But I believe the opposite is true. Authenticity is a strength.

Philosophies of leadership

Every leader has their own philosophy and style. There is no right way to lead. Over time, we found our own philosophies and principles.

Sarah has a practical approach:

> I like to make sure that I can lead from the front. I'm prepared to do the work, but I don't do it because I trust people. I delegate and I empower them to do it. I like to know how to do it because when people have problems, it helps me to be able to support them. You've got to support and trust people. They're highly functioning adults themselves. Some of them have got the potential to go way beyond anything I'm doing, and I would encourage that. Why wouldn't I let them fly?

Joanne wants to be supportive and respectful:

> In terms of thinking about my staff now, I feel like I have a good relationship with my team, but I also demonstrate to them that I'm not afraid to

challenge poor behaviour or poor working practices and that I want them to develop if they want to.

I will offer development opportunities, but we can't force people because actually it doesn't do anybody any good if they are doing a really good job and everybody's happy. And I think management and leadership is often sold as getting people to do their job well, making sure they're happy, and getting them to develop and progress. But it's not always the case that they want to progress, and it's taken me a while, but I feel like I'm getting there with understanding that.

David F. wants to build an independent motivated team:

What I try to be as a manager is someone who, for example, if a member of my team's off, can fill in for them. Particularly in higher education, it's so poorly resourced at times you don't have an option not to. But also that enables me to understand their problems, needs, wants, and gives me the ability to resonate with them. I think I'm pretty hands on as a manager in terms of doing the driving forward.

But once I know team members are up to the level that I would want them to be, I tend to be fairly hands-off and more like a consultant. If you've got a problem, you know that my door's open, you can come and talk to me, and we'll work through it together. I'm really there more to facilitate. It's more about building those qualities with the team, the trust with the team.

I love doing the hands-on stuff, but you have to learn to let go of that and that's a journey to go on as well.

David D. invokes a servant leadership model:

This is going to sound chintzy, and I'm not one who would normally refer to management gurus, but I'm a big lover of Simon Sinek and particularly his 'leaders eat last' philosophy. And what I'm really attracted to is the idea of servant leadership, collaborating with my teams, really getting their input and them feeling like I have their back.

Sometimes I struggle to differentiate that from hero leadership. I do not want to be the guy who's presenteeist where I'm here all the time and I will suffer for you, my team. That's not really what I want to do. It's not what I want to model. But there's so much deep within the psyche that tells you that you should be the one they're all looking up to. So, servant leadership is definitely what I'm aspiring to, but I'm conscious I'm walking a fine line.

I am really keen for my team to feel comfortable talking about their home life, their outside life, never to feel that they have to, but always to feel that they can. Also, I want people to feel that they're in charge of their development with support.

Mehmet takes a strategic and diplomatic approach:

> I think I'm a strategic thinker. I also want others to bring out their strengths and for us to work to high standards, lead the way in the university, show other departments how things can be done by working together. I think people sometimes struggle to link their own work into the objectives. So, the person processing applications, the person on social media promoting the university, what are we all working towards? How can they see the impact of their work in the outputs or outcomes? I think this is a challenge that most people can relate to. I try to give people evidence as a leader by saying: 'Look across the department, this is the impact of our work.' Sometimes that isn't so great, and we use that as a motivating item to say, 'Well, look, the results aren't as anticipated, so how can we do things differently?'
>
> I think, it's about being transparent in a sensitive way and being forward thinking and taking people on that journey with you because you have to invest in people. Because my directors believed in me, they endorsed me. In many ways, I felt like I owed it to them as well not to let them down. So it's a case of trying to impart that into other people at grades four, five, six, seven, trying to show them that by giving them a bit of belief and endorsing their work as well you support them in their work and in trying to be good citizens as well.
>
> I think that sometimes within the tricky area of student recruitment, pressures get really high, especially during clearing. People get a bit thorny with each other. We're in the same team, we're trying to work towards the same outcome. We don't need to be really blunt on emails. We don't need to be really blunt with the way we communicate. People might be having bad days. Let's try to cool down and look at things in a different way.

Dealing with difficult things

Having difficult conversations, dealing with conflict, and supporting underperforming team members is something none of us like doing.

Early in my career, I had a tough moment at work. My head of department noticed that I made a misstep during a meeting. I had cut someone off and consequently they curtly shut me down. Feeling frustrated and cross with myself, I got emotional during the ensuing discussion about the incident. Embarrassed, I just wanted to appear strong. My head of department, however, surprised me. She acknowledged my tears and offered a choice: continue the talk or take a break.

This simple act of giving me ownership over my emotions was incredibly impactful. We ended up having a productive conversation, and it's a lesson I've carried with me. Now, when managing my own team, I use this same approach. Emotions are a part of working life, and offering team members the choice to address them or take a break fosters a supportive environment.

Never assume. Tears or anger can be from frustration or embarrassment as much as hurt feelings or being overwhelmed.

Always have the conversation. The longer you avoid it, the harder it will be.

Resistance

Managing resistance from your direct reports can be challenging, but fostering a sense of ownership and leveraging your interpersonal skills can be powerful in navigating these situations.

Ask open-ended questions to understand the root of their resistance and address any underlying anxieties. Be transparent about the rationale behind decisions and explain how they benefit the team and the organisation. Demonstrate empathy and understanding when addressing concerns and show appreciation for their efforts. By building a solid foundation of trust and respect, you create a safe space for open dialogue and teamwork, making it easier to navigate disagreements constructively.

Instead of being defensive, work together with your team to identify the root cause of the issue and explore potential solutions. This collaborative style fosters a sense of shared responsibility and empowers your team to contribute their unique perspectives and solutions.

Consider offering your team choices within the bounds of the situation. This allows them to feel heard and invested in the outcome. Explain the context and reasoning behind the decision but present the team with options for execution or implementation. This collective approach promotes a sense of ownership and reduces their feeling of being dictated to.

By empowering your team through choice, fostering open and honest communication, building trust and respect, and focusing on problem-solving, you can work towards effective management resistance and create a more engaged and collaborative work environment.

This is not to say you should accommodate any and all challenges or resistance. In the end, you may need to draw a line and set firm directives and accountabilities. This builds on your skills of 'management manners' in communicating well and setting clear expectations.

Addressing performance issues

Managing underperformance or unsatisfactory performance is hard. Early on in my career, I'd see issues in other teams and wonder why things weren't being handled differently. Then I became a manager and realised why – it's tough. Managing performance can be a juggling act: balancing individual needs with team dynamics and organisational goals. Doing this effectively is time-consuming. It takes courage and it requires grit. HR may or may not be helpful. But it's not about punishing those who are not meeting expectations, it's about helping people improve, find satisfaction in their work, and contribute meaningfully.

Sarah explains why it is an important part of being a manager:

> If you don't do it well, then you are seen as weak and any sign of weakness can also be disruptive for your team, because that brings in sort of imbalance and unfairness. You do get a lot of 'That's not fair!' Usually it is fair, but you have to make sure that it appears fair too. I think it is hard. Learning some of those skills early on and recognising that they will develop over time is important, but you've got to tackle poor performance from the start.

Here are some strategies I've learnt from experience that I hope will help you if you are a new manager, navigate the challenges of performance improvement for the first time.

Use the probation period effectively. If possible, you want to identify and address significant competency issues during the probation period. A structured training and development plan during probation, well documented, provides the framework to assess whether someone is suitable to stay in a role permanently.

Start with the 'why' before jumping into the 'how'. You need to establish with the poorly performing team member if there are other reasons for their below par performance at work. Is there a resource, training, or management issue? There might be a situation outside work impacting on their normal functioning. Also try to understand their motivations, their own assessment of their current performance, their ambitions, their expectations, and their aspirations. Opening up this dialogue will enable you to co-create a performance improvement strategy. Whilst you can set out your own expectations as a manager and reference the job description requirements, for a performance improvement action plan to work you need to have buy-in from the staff member. Co-creation of goals will be positively influenced if you understand their personal motivations and circumstances. Set measurable, achievable, and incremental targets. Include training and different support mechanisms in the plan.

Document everything. This is important for both you and your team member's benefit. If you have to bring HR into the situation or formal proceedings are initiated, the process needs to be carried out correctly (according to institutional policy) and recorded appropriately.

Always be consistent and transparent. These two qualities are the fundamentals of good management. They are especially important when it comes to supporting team members with improving their professional performance and meeting the expectations that you have laid out for them. You need to be consistent from the beginning with one-to-ones, appraisals, and target setting. Note, though, that these are not processes that you can suddenly start doing with a poor performer. It is inadvisable for two reasons. Firstly, imposing a new process on them puts them in an unfair position. Secondly, you're giving attention to that person over others in your team who deserve the same support for their professional development.

Be proactive. Do not assume the problem will go away eventually if you ignore it or let the poor practice or behaviours get embedded and ingrained. If you do, resentment will build amongst other team members and the situation is going to be so much harder to undo than if you address to the initial small problems before they grow unwieldy.

Fairness matters. You need to be fair to your whole team. Addressing underperformance supports the rest of your team. It means that they're not unfairly burdened by additional work that they might have to do, by errors that they might have to fix, or the negative consequences of the poor performance of the weak team member. Additionally, it's not fair on them if you have all of your attention on the poor performer. This situation doesn't encourage the other team members to perform well as Joanne reinforces:

> I'm a big believer in challenging poor behaviour and poor practice, especially when it impacts those around them.

Use the frameworks and support around you. Utilise the frameworks of your institution, such as the appraisal and action planning tools that are available. Talk to your HR department to get some support. I've shared some resources at the end of this chapter as extra guidance if you need it. Make use of the experience around you. Build relationships and reach out to other managers in other teams so you can support each other. Reach out to other managers who might have dealt with a similar situation in the past for support and advice. Getting support from others is beneficial to you, not just for your own professional development, but for your emotional and mental resilience as well. As any sort of performance management intervention or challenge within a team is hard on all involved.

Overall, be patient, persistent and celebrate every step of progress. By investing in your team's growth and wellbeing, you'll not only navigate challenges but also cultivate a high-performing and engaged team that drives success for everyone. So be bold, have those tough conversations and set everyone up for success.

Conflict within teams

Solid performance management and communication with your team can go a long way towards preventing conflict building, but it can bubble up for myriad reasons. It is often subtle behaviours that build over time that cause conflict rather than a specific event. Be mindful of developing tension. Encourage your team to talk to you and keep the channels of communication open, confidential, and non-judgemental. Prevention should be your priority.

When mediating on a problem that has arisen, listen to all parties, stick to facts, and focus on behaviours that can be changed.

Unique to our post-COVID-19 hybrid working world and the consequent rise in the use of messaging tools for work are tensions arising from interpretations of 'tone' in written communication. I've experienced a few situations where team members felt offended or upset by the 'tone' of a colleague's message. In many cases, a specific tone was inferred by the reader based on their own context rather than any intention by the sender. It is easy to forget how many contextual clues we take from non-verbal communication which cannot be interpreted objectively in a typed message. To deal with these sorts of conflicts, stick to the facts. Find out what the person wrote. Encourage communication and collaboration between the team members through other means so that they can establish an understanding of each other's work and communication styles.

The middle management sandwich

Middle managers occupy a crucial, yet often demanding, position within an organisation. We act as 'umbrella carriers', shielding our teams from the complexities of higher-level decisions while ensuring their needs are communicated effectively (Gjerde & Alvesson, 2020). This involves filtering information, distilling complex messages into actionable insights for our teams, and translating team concerns into meaningful communication for upper management. Your team want you to represent them in the most positive manner, especially if they are working hard and delivering on their objectives. Jeanette explains:

> I make sure that everyone in both reporting directions knows about the positive feedback, so everyone knows there's a flow of positivity, but the negativity I'm trying to stop. The stuff from above doesn't have to affect the people below, because I outline what the rules are. That way we don't talk about what you can't do, we're talking about what you can do within those rules. So that could be use of budget, that could be a change in systems, or it could be about the team's capacity. It is about understanding in advance how much time the change will take up from everyday work or what the output should be or whatever it may be.

Being a middle manager involves diplomacy, tenacity, and diverse communication styles. It can be challenging, as Simon shares:

> There's a certain level of seniority that you get to where you can't win. One of the things that I did early in my career, but I don't do now, is talk about things being done to us. It's about getting rid of that mythical 'them' or 'they'. It's so important to avoid being disparaging as it's such a cowardly way out and you lose credibility so quickly. If you just say, 'We've got to

do this', or 'This has happened because they've said it will' might make you feel like you're on their side and on their team, but actually quite quickly they won't see you as having any principles. And in the same way, in terms of your senior leadership, if you are always blindly defending your team, it won't go down well. Absolutely, have your team's back. I think that's incredibly important. And they should know that you've got their back. But not to the point where nothing gets challenged and you won't call out poor behaviour and poor performance. They need to trust that you are prepared to tackle the thorny issues as well. I think it's that thing about authenticity. It's about not oversharing and being clear with both your team and your senior managers, but there'll be some things that you can't win. You're going to annoy someone somewhere in this process and you've got to have a thick skin about this.

Yet, being a middle manager also offers an opportunity to shape the direction and wellbeing of teams while contributing to the broader success of the organisation.

A key aspect of the identity of middle managers lies in 'between-ness'. We navigate multiple roles simultaneously, requiring us to:

- **consent** to decisions from senior leadership while ensuring they align with the needs and wellbeing of our teams;
- **cope** with the pressure and conflicting demands from both above and below; and
- **resist** (constructively), when necessary, to advocate for our teams or challenge decisions that might hinder their success (Kond, 1990).

This duality extends beyond the leadership hierarchy. We also serve as bridges between senior leaders, academic colleagues, other departments, and our teams. You'll be negotiating, translating and advocating to ensure alignment with team objectives and organisational goals.

Diplomacy

All that negotiating, translating, and advocating between your team and senior leaders takes consideration and a diplomatic approach. Mehmet advises a considered approach to communicating with senior colleagues:

Think about how things get reported upwards. Thinking about the story and the narrative can be as important as the specific figures or the actual findings of a piece of work say. Applications might be down, but your conversion might be up, so your team is becoming more efficient at processing offers or getting acceptances out of the offers you're making. It is about trying to think up a different angle on things and build something positive off of that. My first key sponsor was in the analytics area. And while it was a fairly technical area one of the most important lessons was on communication. You think about data, and you think about analytics, it's all stats and things like that, but actually it's really about how you can convey that message, talk to others through that story.

Pitching information at the appropriate level is vital, as David F. observes:

I think it's really difficult to be able to articulate something to senior management so that you get what you need without confusing them, and then going back and talking to more tech-y people about the detail. It's about being able to articulate that and knowing the right place to do it, isn't it?

And you won't always manage it, as Julie advises:

Some things are always going to land well, and some things are not going to land well, and that's normal. That's not a sign of your competency or otherwise, it's not a sign of failure. It's just how things are. The trick is learning from what fails and improving on it by reflecting on how you can change your approaches the next time you undertake a change.

To successfully influence decision-making, Mehmet suggests being strategic and drawing on your internal networks:

It's about picking your battles. There might be a way to achieve objectives for all sides of the table, but in slightly different ways. You might have to progress one thing in a different way. I think being confident to push back on some things is really important, but I recognise that not everyone would feel comfortable doing that, especially against senior colleagues. But picking other individuals who might be able to influence them is also productive in this way. You might not feel able to challenge or feel comfortable to push back, but there might be someone else that they're willing to listen to, who you might be able to influence. You could try share your concerns with others and bring the case of that impact at the end.

Whilst we are between senior leaders and our teams, we are also in the middle of our teams and our academic colleagues with whom we collaborate.

Simon finds himself mediating between the two camps on an ongoing basis:

You have to be a broker between the academics and professional services – translating what they want and mean. And also, being able to go back and go, 'Yeah, that's not happening, you're not getting that. But we can do this, we can do that.' And actually, really appreciating the skills of diplomacy. We could just go into every meeting and bang our fists on the table and say, 'This has to be better', 'You have to do this' and 'We expect this from you', but actually you're not ever really going to gain any traction, or you might for one little win, but the longer-term relationships will be damaged. I'm all about relationships and how we foster those, how we maintain those and often how we repair those.

The strategy that I've learned over the years is never say 'no' directly. Instead, I lay out all the challenges and consequences. For example, when a faculty wanted to change their applicant interview pattern from weekly to double the number every other week my team panicked and responded to say that they couldn't process twice the volume in the same amount of time to meet the agreed turnaround time. I didn't simply pass on the answer 'no' or tell the faculty that we couldn't do it. I explained to faculty colleagues that if we were to go ahead, the processing would take twice as long with twice the volume, and therefore our processing timeline would need to be extended and applicants would have to wait longer for a decision. Within half an hour, the faculty had confirmed that they wanted to stick to the current model as it would have a potentially negative impact on conversion to delay notifying applicants of their interview outcomes. But if I had just said no from the outset, the faculty would likely have reacted defensively about their intention. If I had acquiesced without outlining the consequences of the proposal, then there would have been discontent later when applicants didn't get their decisions as fast as previously. When I was at school, I found it annoying that I would be asked to show my workings out, but I now realise that 'showing your workings out' is a helpful strategy for diplomatic negotiation, especially with those who are senior to you.

As a senior academic navigating these same challenges, Peter shares how he has defined his role as a facilitator and broker:

> I think my job is a remover of barriers. I always say to everybody, my entire job is to remove any excuses you have for not doing a fantastic job. My job is to talk to academics and ask what's stopping them from creating a brilliant student experience, doing all these wonderful things, and then liaising with digital learning technologists or professional services or whoever, to ask how we can make sure that we support those academics. Then I go back to the academics, show that we solved a problem and removed those barriers.
>
> If academics are telling me they've got an issue or a great idea, I put them in touch with the right people and ensure that fits in with the whole of the faculty's plan, of the university's plan, and ensure they're speaking to the right people. I always liken it to doing a jigsaw. You need to put everything in place, and somebody has to do the jigsaw and that's my job.
>
> If we see the university as being everybody rather than some monolithic organisation that you can blame for everything, then actually we can move forward.

Digging deeper

Reflect on past experiences with challenging situations (for example, performance issues). What worked well and what could you improve upon?

How can you become more confident and comfortable with early intervention and transparent communication in addressing difficulties?

What leadership skills do you feel you excel at? Conversely, what areas could you use further development in?

Read: McCaffery, P., 2018. *The higher education manager's handbook: effective leadership and management in universities and colleges.* London: Routledge.

Bookmark: CIPD Performance Management Factsheet. This includes a detailed guide to approaching performance management including tools to support it. Available at: www.cipd.org/uk/knowledge/factsheets/performance-factsheet/.

Explore: Indeed, 2023. 14 contemporary leadership theories with explanations. *Indeed*, 22 March. Available at: https://uk.indeed.com/career-advice/career-development/contemporary-leadership-theories.

References

DiGirolamo, J. A. and Tkach, J. T., 2019. An exploration of managers and leaders using coaching skills. *Consulting Psychology Journal: Practice and Research*, 71(3), pp. 195–218. https://doi.org/10.1037/cpb0000138.

Gjerde, S. and Alvesson, M., 2020. Sandwiched: exploring role and identity of middle managers in the genuine middle. *Human Relations*, 73(1), pp. 124–151. https://doi.org/10.1177/0018726718823243.

Kondo, D. K., 1990. *Crafting selves: power, gender, and discourses of identity in a Japanese Workplace.* London: University of Chicago Press.

McCaffery, P., 2018. *The higher education manager's handbook: effective leadership and management in universities and colleges.* London: Routledge.

Peltier, B., 2010. *The psychology of executive coaching: theory and application*, 2nd ed. London: Routledge.

Universities UK (UUK), 2023. Fair admissions code of practice. *UUK*, 9 August. Available at: <https://www.universitiesuk.ac.uk/what-we-do/policy-and-research/publications/fair-admissions-code-practice>.

Walumbwa, F., Avolio, B., Gardner, W., Wernsing, T. and Peterson, S., 2008. Authentic leadership: development and validation of a theory-based measure. *Management Department Faculty Publications*, 24. Available at: <https://digitalcommons.unl.edu/cgi/viewcontent.cgi?article=1021&context=managementfacpub>.

Chapter 8

Reflect, refine, reimagine
Cultivating personal and professional growth

Self-development isn't a destination. It's a continuous journey of growth and improvement as a professional, as a manager, and as a leader.

How do you navigate this path? This chapter challenges the notion that feeling busy justifies neglecting your development or not allocating time for your team. Here, you'll discover strategies for prioritising this crucial investment in yourself and your leadership practice. It delves into the transformative power of reflection, a practice that equips you to learn from experiences, boost confidence, and strengthen relationships.

Members of our community of voices share their struggles and show how they overcame those struggles to become resilient confident leaders.

Looking beyond self-improvement, this chapter explores how to contribute to the collective knowledge of your field. Sharing your expertise isn't just about helping others, it's about stimulating new ideas and contributing to your professional community.

You are not 'too busy'

You have to make time for professional and personal growth. Jeanette addresses how being busy can become an excuse:

> Sometimes we're really busy because we're being directed to certain priorities, but I so often see people just going on and on about how busy they are. So that becomes their truth. The self-talk goes, 'I am really busy, I don't have time for anything else', when actually they're just not using their time properly. This might be because they're micromanaging, they're not delegating when they're not the right person to be doing something that needs to be done by someone else.
>
> People think that with a higher position and a higher grade, you have more work to do or you're more involved in everything, when actually you have a different set of responsibilities and accountabilities, and you should let the experts focus on the work they are good at. You're delivering the message or you're deciding on the strategy, but you shouldn't be in the

DOI: 10.4324/9781003522126-9

system trawling through the data, because you have other people to do that. The director shouldn't be busier than the admissions officer. It's just that the director has a different set of tasks to the admissions officer. So you should be developing your team, leading your team, inspiring, because that is the role of a manager – a leader. It's about ensuring that everyone has what they need and that they can thrive, because that's your role. Your role is helping people to thrive.

If you feel you are too busy, you need to look at your workload. You need to ask: 'What am I doing with my day? Am I being productive? Am I getting involved in things I shouldn't?' If you're too much in the detail, you're probably working 16 hours a day. It's really important to work out why you don't have time and then you make time. Because if you don't want to make time for a team, you shouldn't be a manager.

Prioritising your own development and your management and leadership practice can be managed by a series of short-term adjustments for long-term benefits. Schedule time for specific activities. Prioritise. Evaluate what can be set aside, delegated, or approached differently to give you space for your team and your own development.

Power of reflection

Reflective practice was something I had never engaged with until I had to as part of my PGCert in Higher Education Administration, Leadership and Management, the course I took which is accredited by the Association of Higher Education Professionals (AHEP). I thought reflection was integrated into my everyday approach and was very sceptical about the value of working through reflective models.

I am used to being academically able, articulate, and professionally confident. I initially found reflective practice deeply uncomfortable. It felt too subjective and personal, and way too much effort!

I kept a learning journal for the duration of the course and still use it now. 'Learning journal' is a very grand term for the notebook in which I jot down reflections and observations on an intermittent basis. Keeping a learning journal allows you to record your progress in a non-structured way and to practice thinking and writing reflectively. It doesn't need to be complicated, as Julie explains:

> You can use a journal, you can use notes on your phone, you can use notes on your laptop, whatever works for you. But taking some time on a regular basis and schedule that time to reflect on what's gone well? What hasn't gone well? How could I improve things? What skills have I evidenced? It's really important, and you need to commit to that on a regular basis.

It is a personal document and a reflective account of your experiences.

Why should I try it?

Active reflection (reflective practice) is a way to review and learn from your experiences, actions, and choices. Here are some of the main benefits of reflection:

- Helps you achieve your goals: by reflecting on your progress, you can identify areas where you need to improve and make adjustments to your plans.
- Boosts your self-confidence: when you take the time to reflect on your accomplishments, you start to see your own strengths and abilities. This can give you the confidence to take on new challenges.
- Improves your relationships: reflection can help you to better understand yourself and others. This can lead to more open and honest communication in your relationships.
- Reduces stress: taking the time to reflect on your day and difficult experiences can help you to reduce stress and anxiety.
- Increases creativity: reflection can help you to question your assumptions and to generate new ideas and solutions to problems. This is because it allows you to step back from the situation and see things from an unfamiliar perspective.

How do I do it?

There are lots of different models you can use. I use Jennifer Moon's (2004) model of reflective practice, which follows four steps:

1 Have an experience.
2 Reflect on the experience.
3 Learn from the experience.
4 Try out what you have learnt.

Another popular model that offers a more structured framework is the Gibbs (1988) reflective cycle. It breaks the process of reflection into six stages for you to work through:

1 Describe the experience.
2 Summarise your feelings and thoughts about the experience.
3 Evaluate the experience, both good and bad.
4 Do some analysis to make sense of the situation.
5 Draw conclusions about what has been learned and what could have been done differently.
6 Plan for how to deal with similar situations in the future, or general changes that might be appropriate.

I used these models to get used to reflective practice, but over time, as my confidence has grown, it has become embedded into my professional practice, and I use it more freely and informally. I benefit the most from its use when

I consider a person-focused situation or interaction in my reflections, which I will record in my learning journal. Taking the time to work through the steps and record my reflections slows down my thinking and encourages a close examination of my behaviour, assumptions, and expectations.

You could reflect on training you completed, a situation you faced at work (unexpected or important), or a difficult conversation. Follow the stages of your chosen model. Think about how the experience made you feel, what you took away from it, and what you could do differently next time. You don't need to start at the 'beginning'. However, bonus points for going back and reflecting again for a richer development experience.

I am a quick thinker, so actively slowing my thinking and reflecting on a situation or concept in the moment then returning to it at a later stage has helped me develop a measured, considered approach in my professional practice.

Using reflection to enhance your own practice

Reflection, and the self-awareness it brings, is enormously valuable for enhancing your own professional practice. One of my biggest personal challenges is that I'm a chatterbox, always eager to share my thoughts. But sometimes, my talkative nature can be an obstacle, especially in meetings. Early in my career, I often got into trouble for not controlling my compulsion to interject. I'm still working on it now! There are moments when you need to bite your tongue, even when you have burning questions or brilliant ideas. Timing is crucial, and as team members we must give others the opportunity to share their perspectives.

I worked through this challenge and identified that I needed a mechanism to ensure I didn't forget what I wanted to contribute when I felt it wasn't appropriate to contribute at that moment. I've developed a strategy of jotting down my thoughts. When I feel the urge to interrupt or interject, I quickly write down my ideas in my notebook. This allows me to pause, reflect, and wait for a more appropriate time to contribute. Often, the conversation moves on, or someone else addresses the topic I wanted to bring up. When the chance arises, I can review my list and carefully choose which points to share, ensuring they add value to the discussion in a constructive and structured manner. This also helps me focus on active listening, as I'm not preoccupied with internal debates about what to say. By writing down my thoughts, I can park those ideas temporarily and fully engage in the discussion at hand.

Reflecting to inform intentional choices

At one point in his career, David D. felt a bit stuck and wondered what steps to take to make a change. He found reflection key to identifying his next move:

> I reflected a little bit and I thought, well, where do I want to go next? I want to stay here. I want to continue leading a team. I'm not bothered

about moving up a grade. I want to go back to the centre of the university, probably academic services, maybe the executive office, maybe planning, or something like that. I'd had some coaching from our internal coaching academy at this point which had really helped me identify the three things I might want to do. I thought that maybe I want to work in our Digital and Educational Development team, which is about pedagogical training for academics and support for digital education. I thought there's a couple of schools around the place where I wouldn't mind being ahead of operations, I could do that, schools where the culture attracted me, schools where I knew a few academics and it wasn't too bonkers. And then the final one, I thought, was the academic registrar's office, because they do bits of policy, they're obviously in the centre of things, so maybe I'd fancy a bit of that.

After being a little bit unfulfilled in a previous role and applying for a few jobs that I didn't really think were a good fit, lo and behold, once I narrowed it down to these three areas, a job came up in this very team and it was a sideways move. I think the job at the time was called executive officer. And I went for it, and I got it. Fantastic.

A couple of weeks later my boss said, 'By the way, I'm leaving, would you mind acting up?' I was the only person at that level in the team, so structurally there wasn't anyone else and I was up for it. There was a process, and I got this job formally in February 2022. If I could pick a job in the university and say, 'that's the job for me', it's this one. I love this job. It's bonkers. Some days I think it's the job that's going to kill me, but I love it and it is so varied and so much at the heart of things and I have enough autonomy in how I do things and what I do. It just scratches all of my itches. It is a bit of everything and I'm very happy in my role, which isn't something that a lot of people can say, so I feel very grateful for that.

Resilience

Being careful with yourself and developing strategies for managing stress and staying resilient are important because, as Sarah astutely observes:

It doesn't take much for there to be a bit of a crisis!

We have different degrees of control over factors in our work, and keeping perspective helps focus our energies on what we can control and letting go of what we can't. Stress and anxiety can quickly build if we try to control every element. Imagine three circles:

- **Outermost circle**: Things you might worry about, but can't directly control (weather, politics, others' actions).

- **Middle circle**: Things you can influence through your actions or efforts (work environment, relationships, productivity, your commitments).
- **Innermost circle**: Things you have direct control over (thoughts, choices, actions). (Adapted from Covey, 2013.)

Focus your energy on the middle circle. Don't waste time worrying about what you can't control. Act on things you can influence, even indirectly. Work on letting go of concerns that don't help you (such as blaming others). By focusing on what you can influence, you become more proactive and less stressed. Jeanette shares her thoughts on protecting your mental health in an anxious world:

> You need to be resilient to cope. Doesn't mean you're cold, it doesn't mean you don't care. But it's about choosing what you decide to bring in to stress you out and what you don't. I tell the team quite a lot, if you don't know the outcome, you can prepare for the worst, of course you can. But it hasn't happened yet. It can either go really well or it's going to be a disaster. But neither has happened. Neither is the truth because it's not happened yet. So which one do you choose to believe? You choose to believe that it's going to go really well and it's going to be really positive and it's going to be really fantastic until you find out that it's not, then you deal with it. If you can prepare for it. I can be as prepared as I can be, but a lot of people choose to focus on things that haven't happened yet and they worry about, and they spend so much time stressing. Choose the positive truth, which is that neither is true. So just choose that outcome and believe in it, because if your mind is already thinking of a positive outcome, you're so much more likely to get there.

As managers and leaders, there's this unspoken pressure to be the picture of composure. We're expected to have all the answers, navigate challenges with unwavering calm, and never, ever, show a hint of vulnerability. But that is unrealistic and a recipe for burnout.

Anxiety is a real issue for many of us. I know for a fact it has been for me. It would flare up during high-pressure situations, leaving me with panic attacks and a cocktail of physical symptoms. For far too long, I wore my ability to 'power through' as a badge of pride. Looking back, that was a mistake. I expected too much of myself, and frankly, so did my managers.

Here's the key takeaway: We aren't infallible. And our teams don't expect us to be. In fact, openness about the challenges we face can build trust and connection.

Don't let work worries and concerns take over. There is much talk of work–life balance, which puts work and life in opposition and competition. A mentor once described it to me as finding the balance of work in life, which removes that tension and offers a more holistic approach. What that balance looks like will be different for everyone.

Making mistakes

We all make mistakes. I have made many. You will make many. The best leaders admit their mistakes, own them, fix them (including apologies where required), learn from them, and then move on.

We all beat ourselves up over mistakes, but there is little purpose or value in letting them eat away at your confidence. As Sarah says:

> You cannot be brilliant all the time.

David D. reminds us that, as long as you take ownership to resolve the situation and learn from the experience, you can forgive yourself and let it go:

> Start with the solution. How do we avoid this happening again? And you don't ever need to blame. You never need to blame.

Think about the things you tend to be hard on yourself about. Are there ways to reframe these thoughts in a more positive light? Perhaps you could replace self-critical statements with positive ones that highlight your strengths and capabilities. Remember, we would never speak so critically to a colleague or team member as we do to ourselves. This reframing can help you move away from negative self-talk and foster a more empowered mindset.

When will I know what I'm doing?

I remember when one of my team members told me they looked up to me and hoped to be a manager like me someday. I felt like such a fraud! I smiled, thanked them, said all the usual encouraging stuff, and went away thinking, 'Crumbs, I don't know what I'm doing most of the time!' We often look to others around us and assume they feel more confident and knowledgeable than we do.

I don't think any of us actually know what we're doing a lot of the time. When I make a decision and the team seems to be thinking, 'Wow, she really knows what she's talking about' (yes, we managers can read minds, it's part of our secret cheat code), I usually don't know for sure. The reality is that I, and other managers, operate using a mix of knowledge, experience, risk-based calculated assessment (also known as, intelligent guesswork), and speaking with confidence.

It was a pivotal moment in my management career when I realised that maybe all those people I look up to, the ones who seem so confident and sure of themselves, also question their work, question their worth and struggle with imposter feelings. Magda struggles with feelings of inadequacy often:

> I've always thought that firstly, I'm a non-native speaker, and secondly, I'm not from here so why should anyone listen to anything I have to say, plus what do I have to say? This has not made life easy because there's always

this thought that everybody else is just so much more comfortable in their own skin. Or they pretend that they are, and they come across as confident and knowledgeable.

To those who are just starting out in management, or those considering making the leap, remember that imposter syndrome never truly goes away. We all deal with it, and it's not necessarily a bad thing. It forces us to be more reflective, to acknowledge that we don't know everything and to embrace the value of different perspectives. David D. encourages this reflection:

> Sometimes you look back and see how far you've come, and having those moments is really lovely. I was in the kitchen the other day with one of our apprentices, and she said, 'What have you got on this week? You got anything exciting?' I said, 'Well, not a lot exciting, but I've only got a couple of scary things this week.' And she said, 'What's scary for you?' And inside I'm like, 'Oh, well, it's not everything anymore!' That was a lovely moment, but quite a sobering moment in terms of, crikey, actually maybe everything's going to be all right after all.

Jeanette was someone who challenged me to be brave and continues to encourage us all to be bold:

> If you're brave you can go, 'I'm going to do it, I'm going to try it'. And if you're not scared of failing, so the impostor syndrome isn't kicking in, the sky's your limit, it really is. I always think, 'Right, I've never done this before, but I'm sure I can because I've done all these other things.'

The beauty of a team, and of a wider organisation, lies in collective wisdom and diverse perspectives. Those people you admire for their confidence and apparent expertise likely have their own ways of managing imposter syndrome and self-doubt. Learn from them and don't be afraid to share your own struggles. Together, we can all navigate this challenging aspect of leadership and grow into better managers. Joanne says:

> No one knows everything and everyone started somewhere. But you do find a lot of people who have worked in HE a long time and it sometimes can be intimidating, but just keep asking questions and challenging things. I think for most people in HE, new ideas are always welcome. If you're willing to do the work, then I think the rewards are there for the taking.

Looking beyond

We can all be so focused on our own institutions and specialist disciplines that we might miss what's happening around us. Expanding your view brings new opportunities.

Jeanette shares her philosophy of taking a holistic approach to self-development:

> I do believe in having many strings to your bow and more different things you do, whether that is a hobby or another professional thing that you might jump into. The more strings to your bow you have, the better person you become to employ or to work with or to lead because you develop a wider scope of mind and approach. I've done a lot of coaching and that's one thing that's definitely made me a better leader myself. Through coaching I have learned so much from people that I have coached that I then bring back into my own position and I use when I lead or coach my own staff or myself.

We are higher education professionals who are also school governors, members of sports teams, carers, musicians, coaches, volunteers, campaigners, editors, writers, thinkers, resisters, collaborators, and change makers.

Further study

In an academic environment there is an appreciation of further and higher-level study. Masters' degrees and doctorate programmes can deepen knowledge, enhance research skills, or help you qualify for specific roles and leadership positions. Shorter professional development courses or certificates can provide targeted training in areas, such as online learning, student support services, or educational technology.

David D. reached a point in his career where his lack of an undergraduate degree became a barrier to progression:

> I went for a head of operations job, and I wasn't shortlisted because I didn't have a degree. And my buddy suggested the Postgraduate Certificate in Higher Education Administration, Management and Leadership, as you can do it with 12 months experience in higher education without an undergraduate degree. I was able to make a business case to get funded to do that. I recognise that colleagues who have dependents and care responsibilities may need to be a lot more purposeful and selective about professional development journeys and I really try and support that as far as I can, but I'm conscious I don't have the lived experience. So I went for the PG Cert. I was absolutely daunted going into it and thought I would be the only one there without a degree. But on our cohort of about 38, I would say there were eight or nine of us in the same position, which was great.

Joanne found her professional doctorate gave her credibility in the academic research environment:

> I'm conscious of my accent because I've got quite a strong Yorkshire accent and I think with assumptions around my accent, and working with red brick

universities in particular, having that doctorate gave me some credibility in terms of managing a research centre because I'd gone through the research process myself. I haven't found that anywhere else, to be fair, but working in research it very much was the case. I think it allowed them to see me almost as one of them and to understand it a bit more.

Joanne did, however, find her professional community assumed that doctoral study would mean her moving away from the professional space:

There was a lot of conversations about, well, but you're going to be an academic after this. But I'm like, no, I don't want to be. I'm not doing it for that. I'm doing it, one, because I'm a nerd and I like learning, two, because I want to understand this subject and, three, so I can carry on doing research here and there. I'm never going to be a full-time researcher. That's not what I want. But I want to keep doing bits here and there to understand more.

Consider full-time, part-time, online, or blended learning options to fit your schedule. There are low-cost opportunities, such as degree apprenticeships, internal fee waivers, or in-house courses, but sometimes the most appropriate qualification or programme of study for us incurs a cost. It can be intimidating to make a case for why your employer should invest in your professional development so directly. Magda inspires us to ask for what we need:

What have you got to lose? Be honest. Make a good case. Let them see the potential, let them see what you will bring with this new degree or qualification, whatever it happens to be, let them see it as an investment in you. At the end of the day, it's far better if you keep investing in your staff rather than watching them go and having to go through the recruitment rigmarole all over again.

It can be challenging balance academic study alongside work and other responsibilities. When I first had to for my master's studies, I marvelled at how I could have filled my time as a full-time undergraduate. You have to be organised and strategic. For example, when picking option modules, I considered timings, assessment requirements, and assessment deadlines.

Conferences, workshops, and open lectures entail networking, staying updated on trends, and learning new practices. Free online courses (MOOCs), webinars, and professional association resources offer flexible and accessible learning opportunities. Mentorship, both mentoring and being mentored, offer rich opportunities for professional development and personal growth.

Looking outward

Don't just learn, become a knowledge leader. Academic study, research, and mentoring equip you with valuable knowledge. But why stop there? Share your insights and stimulate debate. Engaging in conferences, publishing articles, or leading workshops allows you to disseminate your knowledge and insights, sparking further discussion and research among others. By applying your knowledge and skills to solve problems and create innovative ideas, you contribute to the advancement of your field and further benefit our communities. Sharing your expertise and experience with others not only empowers them but also helps you solidify and refine your own understanding.

By actively shaping and building knowledge, you create a ripple effect. Your contributions can stimulate debate, inspire new research avenues, and ultimately lead to advancements in knowledge. By sharing your ideas and solutions, you contribute to a collective effort towards progress and innovation, benefiting everyone involved. The process of actively contributing allows you to deepen your understanding, develop critical thinking skills and gain a sense of purpose and fulfilment. Your impact is, and will be, greater than you might think.

Digging deeper

Try using the Gibbs reflective model to work through a challenge you experienced this week and consider how you might approach future similar situations differently.

What specific actions can you take to pursue your learning aspirations? Would pursuing academic study, research, or mentoring others be beneficial?

How can you actively share your experiences and insights to spark further discussions, research, and innovations within your professional community?

Explore: The Reflectors' Toolkit (University of Edinburgh). Available from: www.ed.ac.uk/reflection/reflectors-toolkit. Here you will find resources, models, and questions that can help you start your reflections as well as structuring them.

Watch: The Power of Believing You Can Improve by Carol Dweck (TEDx talk): https://www.ted.com/talks/carol_dweck_the_power_of_believing_that_you_can_improve.

References

Covey, S. R., 2013. *The 7 habits of highly effective people: powerful lessons in personal change*. London: Simon & Schuster.

Gibbs, G., 1988. *Learning by doing: a guide to teaching and learning methods*. Oxford: Further Education Unit, Oxford Polytechnic.

Moon, J. A., 2004. *Reflection in learning & professional development theory & practice*. London: Routledge Falmer.

Beyond survival
Thriving in professional services

If you'd asked me two years ago whether I could write a book, I'd have told you there was no way I could. Authoring books is something other people do. People like my sister who is an English professor. Not me.

But, after finishing the Postgraduate Certificate in Higher Education Administration, Management, and Leadership, I was wondering what challenge to take on next. I was becoming a better manager and professional from my learning and experience. I knew my team would benefit from the work I had done. But I felt unsatisfied. I wanted to give something back to our professional community. I considered blog articles and conference papers, but nothing felt quite right to me. I wanted something that could bridge the gap between the academic world in which I'd studied and the day-to-day reality of the professional services context in which I was working. In November 2023 I sent a voice message to Magda in which I asked: 'What about a book?' From that initial wildly audacious thought, the idea grew legs and a wonderful project evolved. (Please note, this version of events excludes the part where I tried to persuade Magda to do it with me, the hours and hours of work, and the regular existential crises I had about whether I could deliver the final output.)

My hope is for colleagues to see their current, past, and future selves in the stories and advice shared by this book's community of voices. I aspire for the book to ease the professional journey of others, open conversations, make people question norms, and help us reflect.

Here are some of the things I learnt about our professional community through this project.

LinkedIn is a great community for collaboration

LinkedIn was especially important in the success of this project. Higher education is a collaborative community. We can separate commercial sensitivities and work together for the betterment of the sector and our students and staff. We want to do that.

DOI: 10.4324/9781003522126-10

I approached people who had no idea who I was or whether I could write decently, who agreed to be interviewed. I only knew half of the contributors before this project. Only one or two of them knew each other.

I think the eager, positive response I received to this project demonstrates that professional staff and practitioners in higher education are crying out for conversation in this space.

We shouldn't gate-keep knowledge

Sharing knowledge is powerful. The contributors and I learnt all of what we shared through experience and research. An awful lot of it we learnt the hard way, by trial and error, by experience, by failing, and by trying. Why should this keep happening? I believe there's immense value in sharing our accumulated wisdom. By sharing the metaphorical handbook, we can create a more empowering, equitable, and easier experience for everyone.

We need to be confident and speak up

The voices of the professional services community are often drowned out by the weight of academic discourse. When I discussed this book with others across the sector, support and encouragement from my professional services colleagues was swift. They understood the book's purpose: to empower our community. However, navigating the academic space proved more challenging. Some questioned my credibility (I haven't followed the traditional path – perhaps this book is my practical equivalent to a doctoral thesis?) and why the book wouldn't cater to those in teaching and learning roles.

Here's the truth: this book isn't seeking academic validation. It carves out its own space, just as we, the professional services staff, do within higher education. We possess a wealth of expertise and deserve to operate and have our voices heard, both within and outside the academic space. It's time to stop being the quiet voice in the room. We have so much to offer.

So I ask you, what are **you** going to do when you put down this book?

Your commitment

I challenge you to take five small, achievable steps to invest in yourself as a higher education professional. Let's turn the 'I could', 'I might', and 'I should' into 'I can', 'I will', and 'I want to'.

These five suggested prompts offer a foundation for your commitment to your own professional development.

1 Reflect on specific areas where the book's guidance resonated most with your professional journey. Identify one learning point that you want to actively integrate into your professional practice and set yourself a SMART goal linked to it.

2 Identify a skill you'd like to develop to further your career in higher education. Explore specific professional development opportunities (such as courses, projects, workshops, potential mentors) to enable you to enhance this skill. Take a concrete action to make this happen (for example, setting a related goal in your PDP, contacting a potential mentor, raising a proposal with your manager).
3 Consider your existing transferable skills and experiences. How can they be used to address current issues, support others, or spark innovation? Identify an appropriate opportunity to contribute your knowledge and expertise to the collective advancement of your local or sector-wide professional community (such as attending a conference, joining a relevant committee).
4 Reflect on areas in which you lack confidence and identify a specific challenge you'd like to overcome in your professional journey. Develop a plan (which could be seeking mentorship, taking on a new project, or signing up for training) to step outside your comfort zone and prove to yourself you can rise to the challenge.
5 Hold yourself accountable to completing these actions by sharing them with your manager or mentor, including them in your PDP, or sharing them with peers (for example, through internal staff peer groups or online professional networks such as LinkedIn or Twitter using #thrivingHEprofessional).

Your journey

This book has served as a guide, navigating you through the complexities of the UK higher education landscape. From an initial introduction to the sector's history and current debates, you have been equipped with tools to navigate your professional journey, from crafting a development plan to excelling in the application and interview process.

Stepping into leadership positions brings its own set of challenges. This book has provided guidance on nurturing successful teams, fostering trust, and leading through change. We've explored the nuanced role of middle managers, highlighting their crucial role as mediators, negotiators, and relationship builders.

The final chapter has introduced you to reflective practice, a powerful tool for personal and professional growth. By actively engaging in self-reflection and embracing continuous learning, you'll be well-positioned to develop yourself and your team and positively influence the collective knowledge base of higher education. Remember, your contributions and actions will spark further discussions and innovations, creating a ripple effect that benefits everyone within the sector.

Higher education is a dynamic and ever-evolving environment. As you continue your journey, embrace the challenges, celebrate your achievements, and never stop learning. This book is a starting point, empowering you to actively shape your future in higher education and contribute to a thriving and innovative sector.

Value your transferable skills and experience from previous roles. Embrace opportunities for professional development and networking. Don't be afraid to step outside your comfort zone and pursue new challenges. Start conversations. Be open to learning and adapting to new environments.

The direction that you take next is in your hands.

Be bold. Just start.

Index

academic-professional divide 17–22
academic staff 15, 17–22, 33, 64, 66, 91; collaborating with 111–112
academic study and qualifications 122–123
Access and Participation Plan (APP) 15
accountability 38, 63–64, 72, 127; of institutions 16–17; in leadership 101–102, 106
acronyms 23, 33, 54, 60
'admin': as a term 19, 74
anxiety 79, 103, 106, 116, 118–119; about change 94–95, 97; interview 52–53
apprenticeships 12–14, 16, 19, 89, 123
Artificial Intelligence (AI) 48, 87
Association of Higher Education Professionals (AHEP) 31, 42, 60; professional development framework 35–36
authentic leadership 73, 101–103, 110

change: influencing 91–92, 111; managing 73; resistance to 90, 95–97; sector-wide 86–87, 89, 90; supporting your team through 93–95, 97–99
Chartered Institute of Personnel and Development (CIPD) 65, 85, 113
Chartered Management Institute (CMI) 3, 66
collaboration: as a skill 35–36, 50, 67, 72; between academic and professional services staff 19, 21–23, 92, 111–112; between colleagues and peers 31, 40, 60, 92, 125; between universities 17; in leadership 106, 109–111

communication 32–33, 35–37, 48, 67, 102, 116; with senior leaders 79, 92, 110–111; with your team 71–74, 79, 89, 93–99, 105–106, 108–109
confidence 59, 102, 111, 126; building 40–42, 57, 82–83, 116; lack of 7, 120–121; projecting 67 see also skill assessment
contracts 1, 18–20, 55
credibility: developing 34, 42, 63, 122–123, 126; as a leader 78–79, 109–110

debates: in higher education 12–15
decision-making 71, 88, 102; collaborative 90; in higher education institutions 16, 89–90
delegation 80–82, 85, 103, 115
digital literacy 37; in students 13
diplomacy 32, 34, 76, 105, 109–112
Dunbar, D. 71

Education and Skills Funding Agency (ESFA) 16
empowerment: through inclusion 75; in leadership 67, 78–80, 93–94, 98, 102; of others 82, 106, 124, 126; self 37, 40, 120

fair admissions 38, 102
funding: of higher education institutions 12, 16–17, 87, 89; student finance 12

Gibbs, G. 116
globalisation 11, 14
goals see professional development

higher education: history of 10–12
Higher Education Policy Institute (HEPI) 61, 68, 99

Index

Higher Education Role Analysis (HERA) 25–26, 44
Higher Education Statistics Agency (HESA) 16, 18, 23

identity: professional 19–20, 95–96, 98, 110
inclusion 75–78, 85
interview: nerves 52–53; preparation 48–52; presentations and tasks 51–52

job description 35, 44–45, 52, 54; working beyond 57–58, 63

leadership 50–51, 65, 90, 101–102; effective 71; philosophies of 102–105; skills 50, 57–58, 66–68; *see also* authentic leadership
league tables 1, 13
LinkedIn 44, 53, 60, 64, 125–126, 127
listening: as a skill 65, 69–70; for effective communication 32–33, 72, 78, 95–96, 109, 117

management: dotted lines 15–16; manners 71; middle 109–110; of peers 84; one-to-ones 74; team meetings 74
mentoring 64–65, 83–84, 123–124, 127
mission groups 17
mistakes 3, 40, 47, 78, 84, 120
Moon, J. 116

networking: to find a mentor 64; to influence change 91, 93–94, 111; online 127; opportunities for 40; for support 83–84; value of 22, 31, 60, 123

objective setting *see* professional development
Office for Students (OfS) 16, 87

part-time working 76–77
peer support 83–84

performance management 106–108
problem-solving 34, 61–62
professional development: frameworks 35, 37; goal setting 37–39, 41; making time for 114, 123; plan (PDP) 37–38, 127; recording achievements 40–41; self-directed learning 39–40; *see also* skill assessment

Quality Assurance Agency (QAA) 17

reflective practice 62, 74, 115–118; models of 116
regulatory bodies 16–17
Research Excellent Framework (REF) 17
resilience 58, 86, 97–98, 108, 118–119
resistance: from others 90, 106; to change 91, 95–97

secondments 58–60
shadowing 23, 39–42
skill assessment 35–36
social mobility *see* widening participation
study *see* professional development
supporting statement 45–48
sustainability 14, 37

Teaching Excellent Framework (TEF) 17, 87
trust: building 63, 72, 119; in leadership 78–80, 103–104, 106, 110

universities: structure of 15–17; *see also* higher education
University and College Admissions Services (UCAS) 14, 16–17, 60, 87, 89

wellbeing: staff 78, 108, 110; student 14–15
widening participation 13; *see also* Access and Participation Plan (APP)

For Product Safety Concerns and Information please contact our EU
representative GPSR@taylorandfrancis.com
Taylor & Francis Verlag GmbH, Kaufingerstraße 24, 80331 München, Germany

www.ingramcontent.com/pod-product-compliance
Lightning Source LLC
Chambersburg PA
CBHW051543230426
43669CB00015B/2704